4th Teddy Bear & friends Price Guide

by Linda Mullins

Teddy Bear & friends® is a federally registered trademark of Cumberland Publishing, Inc.

Published by Hobby House Press, Inc.
Cumberland, Maryland

Dedication

To all my wonderful friends in the teddy bear world.

Acknowledgements

I have many people and companies to thank for helping me with the preparation of this book. I wish to acknowledge a special debt of gratitude to Marge Adolphson, Barbara Baldwin, Edna Brown, Cynthia Britnall, David Douglass, Jayne Elliott, Jerry Elliott, Vera Fuchs, Gund, Ellen Idema, Ho Phi Le, Barbara Lauver, Jeri Leslie, North American Bear Co., Romy Roeder, Susan Swickard, Lisa Vought, Donna Harrison-West and Susan Wiley.

A special thank you to my friend Georgi Bohrod Rothe for her assistance and professional guidance and to Mary Beth Arkell for her professional computer service. Finally to my publisher for his faith in me which provides me with a means of sharing.

Front Cover
(Left) Steiff Bicolor Bear. Circa 1926. 24in (61cm).
PRICE: N.P.A.
(Right) Steiff Bear. Circa 1907. 24in (61cm).
PRICE: $8000-up
(Center) Steiff Kitty. Circa 1952. 10in (25cm).
PRICE: $125-up
Author's collection (Bears). Colleen Tipton (Kitty).

Title Page
(Left) Steiff Clown. Circa 1910. 17in (46cm).
PRICE: $1200-up
(Center) Steiff Bear. Circa 1907. 28in (71cm).
PRICE: $9000-up
(Right) Steiff Clown. Circa 1910. 13in (33cm).
PRICE: $500-up
(See page 94 for more information.)

Additional copies of this book may be purchased at $12.95
from
Hobby House Press, Inc.
900 Frederick Street
Cumberland, Maryland 21502
or from your favorite bookstore or dealer.
Please add $4.75 per copy for postage.

ISBN: 0-87588-399-0

TABLE OF CONTENTS

HOW TO USE THIS BOOK 4

INVESTING IN TEDDY BEARS AND SOFT TOYS 5

CHAPTER 1 AMERICAN BEARS AND SOFT TOYS........................7

CHAPTER 2 BRITISH BEARS AND SOFT TOYS 34

CHAPTER 3 GERMAN BEARS AND SOFT TOYS..................49

CHAPTER 4 BEARS AND SOFT TOYS OF VARIOUS ORIGIN 140
(Australian, Austrian, French, Polish, Swiss and Japanese)

CHAPTER 5 MECHANICAL BEARS AND ANIMALS 150

CHAPTER 6 MUSICAL BEARS AND ANIMALS 153

CHAPTER 7 ADVERTISING BEARS 156

CHAPTER 8 SMOKEY BEARS 158

CHAPTER 9 ANNALEE CREATIONS 162

CHAPTER 10 RAGGEDY ANN & ANDY DOLLS 167

CHAPTER 11 GOLLIWOGS 172

CHAPTER 12 ARTIST BEARS 177

ABOUT THE AUTHOR 192

HOW TO USE THIS BOOK

This price guide has been arranged as follows:
Country of Origin
Manufacturers in each country (alphabetically)
Bears produced by each manufacturer
Animals produced by each manufacturer
Mechanical Bears and Animals (various manufacturers)
Musical Bears and Animals (various manufacturers)
Advertising Bears (various manufacturers)
Smokey Bear (various manufacturers)
Annalee Creations
Raggedy Ann & Andy Dolls (various manufacturers)
Golliwogs (various manufacturers)
Artist Bears (various American artists)

KEY

KEY FOR ALL BEARS AND ANIMALS

• f.j. indicates "fully jointed" (jointed arms and legs; swivel head).
• n.j. indicates "non-jointed" (unjointed arms and legs; stationary head).
• e.s. indicates "excelsior stuffing" (wood shavings).
• k.p. indicates "kapok stuffing" (a silky fiber which covers the seeds of the tropical kapok tree which grows in Africa, the East Indies and tropical parts of America).
• s.s. indicates "soft stuffing" (stuffed with various soft materials, i.e. cotton, acrylic).
• N.P.A. indicates "no price available" (not enough examples sold to establish price).
• S.A. indicates "still available."

KEY FOR STEIFF BEARS AND ANIMALS

• FF button indicates "STEIFF" name in capital letters with F underscored on pewter colored metal button.
• R.S.B. indicates Steiff name is "raised script" on pewter colored shiny metal button.
• I.B. indicates Steiff name is "incised" in script on shiny chrome button.
• S.L. indicates "stock label" is attached by ear button.
• C.T. indicates "chest tag."

INVESTING IN TEDDY BEARS AND SOFT TOYS

Collecting teddy bears and soft toys is increasing in popularity every year.

The prices in this guide have been determined by studying shows, auctions, printed advertising, prices in newspapers and magazines. By examining the current market, as well as price trends over the last year, I have done my very best to disclose the most up-to-date prices to the best of my knowledge.

However, the current values contained herein should only be used as a guide. The establishment of value must be yours in the end.

Prices may vary due to dealer philosophy and even the whims of the collector himself. For instance, an informed and well-invested collector may choose to pay much more than book value for a piece because it completes a set. Or it may be a collector attends an auction and simply dearly covets a particular piece.

The condition of the bear or animal holds the utmost value in pricing. A piece in mint condition with original manufacturers identification button, label and/or tag will bring a far greater price than one in good or fair condition.

These prices are not absolute. Prices given for the animal pictured take into account the size, condition, identification marks and rarity. Availability also plays a role, as the rarer commands a higher value.

When measuring a bear, do not include the ears. Add value for an unusually large size and/or good condition. Additional value can be established for special appeal or other unique qualities such as color and mechanical performance. Worn, or slightly worn pads can be tolerated by the collectors paying the high prices, but most require excellent fur covering.

Prices shown with the captions in this book are for that particular bear. Every effort has been made for comprehensive representation of most all the genus and species of Teddy Bears known.

Similarly, this guide is not meant to set prices from one region of the country to another.

Neither the author nor the publisher assumes responsibility for any losses which may occur as a result of following this guide.

In summary, no one knows your collection better than you. You must ask yourself if the bear is affordable for you. Do you want it enough to pay the price? If you do, then you have made the right choice.

Tremendously popular among teddy bear collectors of all ages are North American Bear Company's **VanderBear Family**. The Red Flannel Collection was introduced in 1985. The suggested retail price for the entire family (including the unbelievably popular little Muffy) was $172.00. Today the family has sold for as much as $1500.00
Courtesy North American Bear Company.

This group of Steiff teddy bears portrays the special appeal that only comes with generations of love. Adorable as these bears appear, they will not command the price of bears that were not given this same love and attention. Consequently bears in good condition are looked upon by the majority of collectors as a better investment.

Early 1900s Steiff teddy bears are among the most highly sought after collectible bears, commanding the highest prices today. These circa 1907 magnificent 28in (71cm) (pictured on left & right) and 16in (41cm) (center) bears have increased in value considerably in the last decade. Limited production, age, condition and facial expression are the major factors to be considered when determining value.

CHAPTER 1
AMERICAN BEARS AND SOFT TOYS

Aetna

Circa 1908. 20in (51cm); Dense pinkish beige mohair; glass eyes; f.j.; e.s.; cardboard underlines felt foot pads; stamped on foot "AETNA." Rare.
CONDITION: Mint   **PRICE:** $3000-up
Courtesy Barbara Baldwin.

Applause

Robert Raikes Creations. First Edition. 1985. Limited edition of 7500 of each design. Carved wooden faces; acrylic plush; plastic eyes; f.j.; s.s.
(Front row left to right)
Huckle Bear. 22in (56cm).
CONDITION: Mint   **PRICE:** $275-up
Sebastian. 22in (56cm).
CONDITION: Mint   **PRICE:** $275-up
Eric. 14in (36cm).
CONDITION: Mint   **PRICE:** $625-up
Rebecca. 22in (56cm).
CONDITION: Mint   **PRICE:** $675-up
(Back row left to right)
Bently. 14in (36m).
CONDITION: Mint   **PRICE:** $300-up
Chelsea. 14in (36cm).
CONDITION: Mint   **PRICE:** $950-up
Courtesy Applause.

Robert Raikes Creations. Second Edition. 1986. Limited edition of 15,000 of each design. Carved wooden faces; acrylic plush; plastic eyes; f.j.; s.s.

(Front row left to right)
Penelope. 16in (41cm).
CONDITION: Mint
PRICE: $550-up
Christopher. 16in (41cm).
CONDITION: Mint
PRICE: $350-up
Benjamin. 16in (41cm).
CONDITION: Mint
PRICE: $375-up
(Back row left to right)
Max. 24in (61cm).
CONDITION: Mint
PRICE: $200-up
Kitty. 24in (61cm).
CONDITION: Mint
PRICE: $200-up
Tyronne. 36in (91cm). Limited edition of 5000.
CONDITION: Mint
PRICE: $750-up
Arnold. 24in (61cm).
CONDITION: Mint
PRICE: $225-up
Courtesy Applause.

Bruin Manufacturing Company

(B.M.C.). Circa 1907. 16in (41cm); off-white long silky mohair; glass eyes; tan-colored stitched nose; f.j.; excelsior and kapok stuffing; woven label on foot reads: "B.M.C." Rare.
CONDITION: Excellent
PRICE: $2800-up
Courtesy Barbara Baldwin.

Character Novelty Co.

(Left) Circa 1950. 23in (58cm); white mohair; blue glass eyes; f.j.; s.s.; black airbrushed claws; label in ear reads "Designed by Character;" chest tag reads: "A Character Toy Made in U.S.A./ Character Novelty Co., Inc., N.Y.C." Information regarding stuffing and materials is also printed on tag.
CONDITION: Mint   **PRICE:** $300-up
(Right) Ideal Bear. Circa 1940. 10in (25cm); cinnamon-colored mohair; glass eyes; black hard resin nose; red felt tongue; n.j.; s.s.; paper hang tag reads: "An Ideal Ultrafine Animal/Ideal Novelty & Toy Co. (Stuffed Toy Division) Long Island City, N.Y.
CONDITION: Excellent   **PRICE:** $100-up
(Front) Bear. Circa 1950. 10in (25cm); bright gold-colored mohair; shoe-button eyes backed with white felt circles; red felt tongue; f.j.; k.s.; black airbrushed claws; label in ear reads: "Designed by Character/So. Norwalk Conn."
CONDITION: Excellent   **PRICE:** $100-up

(Left) Bear. Circa 1950. 13in (33cm); beige mohair; in-set short mohair snout; shoe-button eyes backed with white felt circles; n.j.; s.s.
CONDITION: Excellent   **PRICE:** $75-up
(Right) Bear. Circa 1950. 10in (25cm); cinnamon-colored mohair; shoe-button eyes backed with white felt circles; n.j.; s.s.
CONDITION: Excellent   **PRICE:** $100-up
Courtesy Marge Adolphson.

Circa 1960. (Left) 19in (48cm); (Right) 15in (38cm); long cinnamon synthetic plush; plastic eyes; f.j.; s.s. Label sewn into ears reads: "Designed by Character." Reverse side of label reads: "Character Novelty Co., Inc./So. Norwalk, Conn."
CONDITION: Excellent **PRICE:** (Left) $65-up
                                     (Right) $50-up
Courtesy Marge Adolphson and Donnella Summers.

Commonwealth Toy and Novelty Co.

Feed Me Bear. Circa 1937. 16in (40.6cm); cinnamon-colored mohair; glass eyes; n.j.; k.s. When the ring located on top of head is pulled, the mouth opens and dry foods and candy are swallowed. The food can then be removed by opening a zipper at the back of the bear, disclosing a metal compartment where the food is stored, without harming the bear. Originally came with a bib and a lunch box. The National Biscuit Co. used the bears to advertise their animal crackers.
CONDITION: Fair   PRICE: $450-up

Gund

This 100 year old company is still run by descendants of its first employee.

Gund claims it jumped on the teddy bear wagon in 1906. In 1917 the company advertised dolls and toys which walked, waddled, tumbled, danced and crept.

When Adolph Gund sold the business to his protégé Jacob Swedlin, the firm continued to prosper with a line of velveteen animals that did acrobatics in 1927.

The "Regal" line of plush animals with molded faces and moving eyes were popular in the 1940s and 1950s, as were floppy, sleepy animals called Dreamies.

In the 1950s Gund was the largest stuffed toy maker in the United States, producing a number of Disney characters which are quite collectible today.

Important components of Gund products today are the "Collector Classics" and "Signature Collection."

Rumble Baby Bear. Circa 1950. 15in (38cm); rust-colored plush body; beige plush lined ears; molded vinyl face; plastic sleep eyes; n.j.; k.s. manufacturer's identification label sewn into seam of arm.
CONDITION: Mint   PRICE: $125-up
Courtesy Janice Penny.

(Left to right) Circa 1950. 10in (25cm); black and white synthetic plush; soft vinyl molded face; plastic sleep eyes; n.j.; s.s. Label sewn into side seam reads: "Gund Mfg Co/A Swedlin Inc.,/N.Y. N.Y."
CONDITION: Excellent   **PRICE:** $75-up
Cubbie Bear (Standing on all fours). Circa 1950. 12in (31cm) cinnamon and gold synthetic plush; soft vinyl molded face; painted eyes; n.j.; s.s. Label sewn into seam of leg reads: "Cubbie Gund/ Gund Mfg Co.,/A Gund Creation."

CONDITION: Excellent   **PRICE:** $45-up
Cubbie Bear. Circa 1950. 13in (33cm); dark brown acrylic plush; soft vinyl molded face; painted eyes; n.j.; s.s.; dress and shoes an integral part of body; removable apron. Label sewn into seam of leg reads: "Cubbie Gund/Gund Mfg Co.,/A Gund Creation."
CONDITION: Excellent   **PRICE:** $65-up
Courtesy Donnella Summers.

Circa 1950. Sizes range 11in (28in) to 16in (41cm); various shades of brown and white synthetic plush; soft vinyl molded snouts; plastic eyes; n.j.

(first bear in back is fully jointed); s.s. Gund's identification label sewn into seam of bears.
CONDITION: Good   **PRICE:** $35 - $50-up
Courtesy Marge Adolphson and Donnella Summers.

The *Gundy™Collection.* 1983 to 1991. (Left to right): *Anniversary Bear.* 1983. $165-up *Gundy Bear.* 1984. $95-up *Gundy Bear.* 1985. $75-up *Gundy Bear.* 1986. $50-up *Gundy Bear.* 1987. $125-up The story of *Gundy™* began in 1983. It is an official beginning because the bear that is considered the first *Gundy™* was actually the 1983 *Anniversary Bear™.* The *Anniversary Bear™*, an 8in (20cm) f.j. bear with leatherette paw pads and a specially embroidered anniversary label, celebrated Gund's 85th year of bear making since 1898. It was so well received that in 1984 the first Gundy collectible bear was introduced. Each later version of Gundy has different plush fabrics and variations of trim, accessories and display box. All *Gundy's™* stand 9in (25cm) tall and are f.j. An attractive display box enhances the collectibility. *Gundy™* is an annual edition. The production of *Gundy™* is limited to the year in which it is introduced. *Courtesy Gund.*

Canterbury Collection. *Montague.* 1992. 13in (33cm); black English alpaca body; red mohair head; plastic eyes; f.j.; s.s.; red and black ribbon with feather on left shoulder. Limited edition 750.
CONDITION: Mint   **PRICE:** $135-up
Courtesy Gund.

Pawtucket™ 1991. 20in (51cm); brown acrylic plush; buckskin lined open mouth and inner ears; plastic eyes; f.j.; s.s; leather nose and paw pads. Limited edition of 840 produced one year only. *Pawtucket*™ is from Gund's Signature Collection.
CONDITION: Mint   PRICE: $375-up
Courtesy Gund.

(Left) **Unmarked American manufacturer** (probably Gund). Rabbit. Circa 1930. 13in (33cm); blue artificial silk plush; pink glass eyes; jointed arms; stationary legs and head; e.s.; original felt and cotton clothes.
CONDITION: Excellent   PRICE: $165-up
(Center) Rabbit. Circa 1930. 18in (46cm); white mohair; pink glass eyes; jointed arms; stationary legs and head; e.s.; original felt and cotton clothes.
CONDITION: Excellent   PRICE: $250-up
(Right) **Unmarked American manufacturer** (probably Gund). Rabbit. Circa 1930. 13in (33cm); pink artificial silk plush; pink glass eyes; jointed arms; stationary legs and head; e.s.; original felt and cotton clothes.
CONDITION: Excellent   PRICE: $165-up
Courtesy Margaret Benike.

Hecla

Circa 1907. 18in (46cm); white mohair; glass eyes; f.j.; e.s.; brown stitched nose and claws. Rare.
CONDITION: Mint   PRICE: $750-up
Courtesy Barbara Baldwin.

The Ideal Toy Company

Legend has it that in 1902, when Ideal founder Morris Mitchom saw the now famous Clifford Berryman cartoon of President Roosevelt's encounter with a bear, he convinced his wife to create a little teddy bear by hand. The cuddly bear was an instant winner.

That first little bear, hand-stuffed with excelsior, is credited with receiving Teddy Roosevelt's approval in 1902. Since that time, Ideal's production plant grew to more than 4000 employees worldwide. However, when the company was sold to CBS in 1982 the teddy bear was no longer part of the picture.

Even though no concrete proof of identification was used for early Ideal bears, there is a consensus as to recognizable Ideal features: wide, triangular head; large, wide-apart ears; short mohair, pointed pads on feet and fairly long and slender bodies.

Since the 1950s and 1960s were an era of prolific production by Ideal, many bear collectors today owned these charming creatures during their own childhood.

A familiar feature of bears of this era are molded vinyl faces with painted features. Many had adorable big sleep eyes. Most were unjointed with chunky soft bodies of rayon plush.

Circa 1907. 18in (46cm); off-white mohair; shoe-button eyes; f.j.; e.s. Rare early design.
CONDITION: Excellent   PRICE: $3200-up
Courtesy Barbara Baldwin.

(Left) Circa 1907. 18in (46cm); honey-colored mohair; shoe-button eyes; f.j.; e.s.
CONDITION: Excellent
PRICE: $2000-up
(Right) Circa 1907. 16in (41cm); black dense wool plush; shoe-button eyes; f.j.; e.s.; red (faded pink) stitched mouth and claws. Rare color.
CONDITION: Excellent
PRICE: $2300-up
Courtesy Barbara Baldwin.

Circa 1907; 16in (41cm); gold mohair; shoe-button eyes; f.j.; e.s.
CONDITION: Excellent   PRICE: $1500-up
Courtesy Ho Phi Le.

Circa 1907. 15in (38cm); silky rich gold colored mohair; shoe-button eyes; f.j.; e.s.; arms set low; large ears. Rare.
CONDITION: Excellent   PRICE: $1600-up
Courtesy Le Day.

(Left) Circa 1907. 12in (31cm); short gold mohair; glass eyes; f.j.; e.s.
CONDITION: Excellent
PRICE: $1400-up
(Right) Circa 1907. 6in (15cm); honey-colored mohair; painted googly-type eyes; f.j.; e.s. Rare.
CONDITION: Excellent
PRICE: $1400-up

(Left) Circa 1940. 14in (36cm); cinnamon-colored synthetic plush; white synthetic plush snout, lining of ears and paw pads; black plastic nose; glass eyes with white plastic betzal around eyes; red felt tongue; f.j.; s.s. Label sewn into seam of body reads: "It's A Wonderful Toy/It's Ideal/Made in USA by Ideal Toy Co."
CONDITION: Excellent   **PRICE:** $95-up

(Right) Circa 1940. 12in (31cm); white synthetic plush; cinnamon-colored synthetic plush lined ears; red and check cotton outfit an integral part of body; black plastic nose; plastic eyes; red felt tongue; n.j.; s.s. Label sewn into seam reads: "It's A Wonderful Toy/It's Ideal/Made in USA by Ideal Toy Corp."
CONDITION: Excellent   **PRICE:** $45-up
Courtesy Marge Adolphson and Donnella Summers.

Musical Clown Bear. Circa 1950. 15in (38cm); cinnamon-colored synthetic plush; white with brown spots synthetic plush trousers, paw pads and lining of ears; yellow felt hat; molded soft vinyl face; plastic eyes; n.j.; s.s. Label stitched in seam of shoulder reads: "It's a Wonderful Toy/It's Ideal." Music (Brahm's Lullaby) is activated by moving right paw in downward position. Ideal produced numerous appealing designs with vinyl faces during the 1950s to 1960s era.
CONDITION: Mint   **PRICE:** $100-up
Courtesy Donnella Summers.

Knickerbocker Toy Co.

The Knickerbocker Toy Co. originated in New York as a manufacturer and seller of stuffed dolls, animals, toy puppets, marionettes and mechanical toys.

In 1979, the company was sold to Lionel, which went bankrupt itself five years later.

Louis and Tammy Knickerbocker (no relation) resurrected the Knickerbocker tradition and began marketing a quality line of Knickerbocker products in January 1990.

(Left) Circa 1930. 17in (43in); white mohair; white velveteen paw pads; green glass eyes; "metal" nose; f.j.; e.s. head; s.s. body.
CONDITION: Excellent
PRICE: $300-up
(Right) Circa 1930. 11in (28cm); white mohair; white velveteen paw pads; green glass eyes; black stitched nose; f.j.; e.s. head; s.s. body.
CONDITION: Excellent
PRICE: $225-up
Courtesy Marge Adolphson.

Circa 1940 to 1950. Sizes range from 13in (33cm) to 20in (51cm); beautiful long silky mohair; short mohair in-set snout (Circa 1940. 20in [51cm]), velveteen in-set snout (Circa 1950. 13in [33cm] to 18in [46cm]); velveteen paw pads; f.j.; s.s. Knickerbocker identified their bears with a label sewn into the seam of the body. The label reads "Knickerbocker Toy Co. Inc./New York." Reverse of label reads: "Animals of Distinction/ Made in U.S.A."
CONDITION: Excellent
PRICE: Ranges from $250 to $500-up

(Left) Circa 1950. 11in (28cm); blonde mohair; in-set beige cotton snout; appliqued black velveteen nose; no paw pads; glass eyes; unjointed arms and legs; swivel head; unusual large beige felt lined ears; s.s.
CONDITION: Good   PRICE: $85-up
(Center) Circa 1950. 11in (28cm); gold silk plush; short white silk plush in-set snout; beige velveteen pads; plastic eyes; f.j.; s.s. Label sewn into side seam reads: "Joy of a Toy Knickerbocker. Old Fashioned Jointed Teddy."
CONDITION: Good   PRICE: $75-up
(Right) Circa 1950. 14in (36cm); bright gold mohair; beige velveteen in-set snout; appliqued black velveteen nose; replaced eyes (original eyes were glass); beige velveteen paw pads; f.j.; s.s.
CONDITION: Good   PRICE: $125-up
Courtesy Jeanne A. Miller.

OPPOSITE PAGE:
(Left) Knickerbocker Bear Company. *Brumm Bear.* 1992. 18in (46cm); beige-colored distressed mohair; black button eyes; f.j.; s.s. Limited edition of 1000; hand numbered; comes with a Knickerbocker signature pin.
CONDITION: Mint   PRICE: $250-up
(Right) *Mitchom.* 1992. 12in (31cm); gold acrylic plush; black glass eyes; f.j.; s.s.. Limited edition of 1000; hand numbered; comes with a Knickerbocker signature pin.
CONDITION: Mint   PRICE: $70-up
Courtesy Knickerbocker Bear Company.

(Left) Knickerbocker Toy Co. Yogi Bear. 1959. 17in (43cm); brown acrylic plush; gold acrylic plush chest; plastic molded face and hands; painted features; turquoise blue felt hat; n.j.; s.s.; label sewn into tummy seam reads: "Knickerbocker Toy Co., Inc./New York, U.S.A./Washable." Reverse of label: "HUCKLEBERRY HOUND Toy." Originally came with tie.
CONDITION: Excellent   PRICE: $50-up
(Center) Knickerbocker Toy Company. Bear. Circa 1935. 22in (56cm); cinnamon-colored mohair; glass eyes; f.j.; k.s.
CONDITION: Excellent   PRICE: $400-up
(Right) Knickerbocker Toy Company. "Musical" Bear. Circa 1960. 15in (38cm); gold acrylic plush; beige felt in-set snout; black plastic eyes; brown felt nose; f.j.; s.s.; label attached to chest reads: "Animals of Distinction/Made in U.S.A.," reverse of label reads: "Knickerbocker Toy Co. Inc./New York. Music is produced by turning handle at side of bear."
CONDITION: Good   PRICE: $175-up

North American Bear Co.

A company which has expanded immensely over the past few years is the North American Bear Co. A journalist, Barbara Isenberg, founded this company in 1978, when she created *Albert, The Running Bear*. This sweat-suit dressed bear is the subject of three books and still an important part of the company's product line.

The still old-fashioned, but brightly-colored VIB (Very Important Bear) line commands market rates of over $1000 by collectors of the company's products.

After these impressive teddies came the *VanderBears*, a family of teddies dressed in Edwardian period clothing. The very smallest of these whimsical creatures is called *Muffy*. She was born in 1984 and was presented in a christening gown. It took awhile for this "Barbie" of the bear world to take hold, but once she did, her popularity has been unsurpassed.

Very Important Bears (V.I.B.'s). *Cinbearella.* 1991. 22in (56cm); turquoise velveteen-type material; plastic eyes and nose; n.j.; s.s. Dressed in pink satin dress carrying a tiny jointed mouse (6in [15cm]) in each pocket. Limited edition of 750. Tag attached to bear reads: "North American Bear Company, Inc. Exclusively Distributed by Walt Disney World®."
CONDITION: Mint   **PRICE:** $300-up

The Taffeta Holiday Collection. Introduced 1986. Retired 1988. ORIGINAL SUGGESTED RETAIL PRICE: $197 **1993 PRICE GUIDE:** $1650-up *Courtesy North American Bear Company.*

The Nutcracker Suite Collection. Introduced 1987. Retired 1988.
ORIGINAL SUGGESTED RETAIL PRICE: $207
1993 PRICE GUIDE: $1200-up
Courtesy North American Bear Company.

NORTH AMERICAN BEAR COMPANY

VERY IMPORTANT BEARS (V.I.B.'s)

NAME OF EDITION	INTRODUCED	RETIRED	1993 PRICE GUIDE
AMELIA BEARHART			
(first outfit [pink])	1980	1983	$1500-up
(second outfit [tan])			$1200-up
SCARLETT O'BEARA I	1980	1984	$450-up
ANNA BEARVLOVA	1981	1987	$275-up
BEARISHNIKOV			
(first outfit [white])	1981	1983	$1100-up
(second outfit [light blue])			$1000-up
WILLIAM SHAKESBEAR	1981	1988	$400-up

NAME OF EDITION	INTRODUCED	RETIRED	1993 PRICE GUIDE
GREEN BEARET			
(first outfit [army green])	1982	1983	$1100-up
(second outfit [hunter green])			$600-up
BJORN BEARG	1982	1984	$500-up
QUEEN ELIZABEAR	1983	1987	$300-up
HUMPHREY BEARGART I	1983	1988	$275-up
LUDWIG VON BEARTHOVEN	1983	1984	$500-up
KAREEM ABDUL JABEAR	1984	1985	$650-up
ELVIS BEARSLEY	1984	1985	$450-up
AUDREY HEPBEARN	1986	1988	$300-up
BLACKBEARD	1986	1990	$250-up
EBEARNEEZER SCROOGE	1988	1988	$400-up

Prices are for bears in mint condition with original accessories (where applicable).

NORTH AMERICAN BEAR COMPANY

VANDERBEARS & MUFFY

NAME OF EDITION	SIZE	INTRODUCED	RETIRED	ORIGINAL SUGGESTED RETAIL PRICE	1993 PRICE
THE VANDERBEAR					
FAMILY (Undressed)		1983			
Cornelius	20in (51cm)			$36.00	$45.00
Alice	18in (46cm)			$30.00	$42.00
Fluffy	12in (31cm)			$18.00	$27.50
Fuzzy	12in (31cm)			$18.00	$27.50
Muffy	7in (18cm)	1984 (Spring)		$12.00	$17.50

The VanderBear Family are fully jointed with hand-stitched noses, rich golden plush and felt paws. Early bears had manufacturer's label sewn into seam at base of body ("tush tag"). Later, tags were sewn into seam of upper torso.

NAME OF EDITION	SIZE	INTRODUCED	RETIRED	ORIGINAL SUGGESTED RETAIL PRICE	1993 PRICE
THE CLASSIC VELVET					
COLLECTION		1983	1988		
Cornelius				$48.00	$125-up
Alice				$46.00	$120-up
Fluffy				$30.00	$100-up
Fuzzy				$30.00	$100-up
Muffy Christening		1984 (Spring)	1985	$18.50	$350-up
(First outfit [not removable])					
THE RED FLANNEL		1985	1988		
COLLECTION					
Cornelius				$48.00	$300-up
Alice				$46.00	$300-up

NAME OF EDITION	SIZE	INTRODUCED	RETIRED	ORIGINAL SUGGESTED RETAIL PRICE	1993 PRICE
Fluffy				$30.00	$200-up
Fuzzy				$30.00	$225-up
Muffy				$18.00	$525-up
Muffy Valentine I		1986	1989	$20.00	$300-up
THE CRUISEWEAR COLLECTION		1986			
Cornelius			1988	$53.00	$195-up
Alice			1988	$47.00	$165-up
Fluffy			1988	$31.00	$125-up
Fuzzy			1988	$31.00	$125-up
Muffy			1991	$18.50	$95-up
THE TAFFETA HOLIDAY COLLECTION		1986	1988		
Cornelius				$51.00	$250-up
Alice				$56.00	$400-up
Fluffy				$35.00	$400-up
Fuzzy				$33.00	$175-up
Muffy				$22.00	$495-up
Muffy Halloween Witch		1986	1988	$20.00	$450.00
THE DAY IN THE COUNTRY COLLECTION		1987			
Cornelius			1989	$55.00	$150-up
Alice			1989	$51.00	$250-up
Fluffy			1989	$34.50	$125-up
Fuzzy			1989	$34.50	$125-up
Muffy			1991	$21.50	$75-up
THE NUTCRACKER SUITE COLLECTION		1987	1988		
Cornelius				$54.00	$200-up
Alice				$58.00	$275-up
Fluffy				$37.00	$175-up
Fuzzy				$35.00	$125-up
Muffy				$23.50	$495-up
THE SAFARI COLLECTION "OUT OF IT IN AFRICA"		1988	1991		
Cornelius			1991	$65.00	$100-up
Alice			1991	$60.00	$100-up
Fluffy			1991	$45.00	$100-up
Fuzzy			1991	$42.50	$125-up
Muffy			S.A.	$25.00	$25-up
THE SKATING COLLECTION "FURRIER AND IVES"		1988	1989		
Cornelius				$70.00	$150-up
Alice				$67.00	$150-up
Fluffy				$44.00	$120-up
Fuzzy				$40.00	$125-up
Muffy				$28.00	$300-up
Muffy Valentine II		1989	1991	$24.50	$75-up

NAME OF EDITION	SIZE	INTRODUCED	RETIRED	ORIGINAL SUGGESTED RETAIL PRICE	1993 PRICE
THE HIGH TEA COLLECTION	1989		1992		
Cornelius				$63.00	$100-up
Alice				$60.00	$125-up
Fluffy				$38.00	$75-up
Fuzzy				$37.00	$75-up
Muffy			S.A.	$28.00	$28-up
Muffy Angel	1989		1989	$40.00	$195-up
THE TREE TRIMMING COLLECTION	1989		1989		
Cornelius				$70.00	$140-up
Alice				$63.00	$140-up
Fluffy				$42.00	$120-up
Fuzzy				$36.00	$120-up
Muffy				$28.50	$225.00
Scotty VanderDog				$9.00	$95-up
Muffy's Cookie Plate				$6.00	$95-up
Christmas Tree				$50.00	$300-up
BACK TO SCHOOL	1990				
Muffy			S.A.	$31.00	$31-up
Hoppy VanderHare				$31.50	$31-up
Muffy's School Desk		1991	1991	$22.00	$85-up
Muffy's Trunk		1991	1991	$28.00	$125-up
THE VICTORIAN SLEEPWEAR COLLECTION	1990		1992		
Cornelius				$58.00	$100-up
Alice				$59.00	$100-up
Fluffy				$39.00	$75-up
Fuzzy				$36.00	$75-up
Muffy			S.A.	$30.00	$30-up
Muffy's Teddy		1990	1992	$5.00	$15-up
THE PURPLE VELVET COLLECTION MUSICAL SOIRÉE	1990		1992		
Cornelius				$84.00	$100-up
Alice				$74.00	$100-up
Fluffy				$48.00	$75-up
Fuzzy				$46.00	$75-up
Muffy			1992	$34.00	$40-up
Muffy's Violin			1991	$12.00	$95-up
Musical Soirée Family Tree		1992		$60.00	$100-up
Muffy Little Fir Tree (SPECIAL BOXED EDITION)		1990	1990	$44.00	$225-up
Muffy Snowbear		1991	1991	$46.00	$95-up

Prices are for bears in mint condition with paper tag and original box.

Unidentified American Manufactured Bears and Animals

(Left) Electric-Eye Cat. Circa 1930. 10in (25cm) long by 6in (15cm) tall; pale yellow rayon plush; eyes are small flat light bulbs; n.j.; eyes light up and flicker when tail is turned.
CONDITION: Excellent   **PRICE:** $300-up
(Center) Electric-Eye Bear. Circa 1907. 20in (51cm); cinnamon-colored mohair; eyes are small flat light bulbs; f.j.; e.s. Eyes light up by pressing button concealed in tummy of bear.
CONDITION: Excellent   **PRICE:** $1000-up
(Right) **National French Fancy Novelty Co.** *Sleeping Toodles.* Dog. Circa 1924. 10in (25cm) long by 8in (20cm) high. White and gold mohair; sleeping celluloid eyes (eyes close like a sleeping doll when laid in sleeping position); unjointed legs; swivel head.
CONDITION: Excellent   **PRICE:** $400-up

(Left) Electric-Eye Bear. Circa 1907.
22in (56cm); red, white and blue mohair; eyes are small flat bulbs; jointed
arms; stationary head and legs; e.s.
Eyes light up by pressing button in
back of upper torso.
CONDITION: Excellent
PRICE: $850-up
(Right) Electric-Eye Bear. Circa
1907. 19in (48cm); white mohair;
eyes are small flat bulbs; jointed
arms; stationary legs and head; e.s.
Eyes light up by pressing button at
side of torso.
CONDITION: Excellent
PRICE: $750-up
Courtesy Sherryl Shirran.

Circa 1909. 30in (76cm); deep
gold-colored mohair; shoe-button
eyes; f.j.; e.s. Early clothes not
original to bear.
CONDITION: Good
PRICE: $3000-up
Courtesy Denise Grey.

Circa 1909; 12in (31cm); short gold mohair; glass eyes; f.j.; kapok and excelsior stuffing. Clothes not original. One of the winning bears chosen for the 1986 Workman Calendar Contest.
CONDITION: Good   PRICE: $750-up
Courtesy Donna Harrison-West.

(Left) Circa 1910. 12in (31cm); honey-colored mohair; glass eyes; unusual stitched nose; f.j.; e.s.
CONDITION: Excellent   PRICE: $1100-up
(Center) Circa 1910. 15in (38cm); short golden tan mohair; shoe-button eyes; brown stitched nose, mouth and claws; f.j.; e.s.
CONDITION: Excellent   PRICE: $1100-up
(Right) Circa 1910. 12in (31cm); light beige mohair; shoe-button eyes; black fabric nose; f.j.; e.s.
CONDITION: Good   PRICE: $1200-up

Long-Voice Toy Bear. Circa 1914. 10in (25cm); gold mohair; glass eyes; jointed arms; swivel head. When toy is released after being pressed down, it emits a long, drawn-out squeal from voice box concealed in body.
CONDITION: Good   PRICE: $450-up
Private collection.

Circa 1915. 15in (38cm); blonde mohair; glass eyes (color painted on back);
brown stitched nose, mouth and claws;
f.j.; e.s.
CONDITION: Good
PRICE: $875-up
Courtesy Denise Grey.

(Left) Circa 1915. 13½in (34cm);
short pale gold mohair; shoe-button
eyes; brown cotton twill in-set nose;
f.j.; e.s.
CONDITION: Good
PRICE: $250-up
(Right) Circa 1915. 15in (38cm); short
rust-colored mohair; shoe-button eyes;
sliced-in ears; f.j.; e.s.
CONDITION: Good
PRICE: $295-up
Courtesy Marge Adolphson.

(Left) Circa 1920. 12in (31cm); deep gold-colored mohair; glass eyes; black fabric nose; f.j.; e.s.
CONDITION: Good   PRICE: $550-up
(Center) Circa 1910. 8in (20cm); short gold-colored mohair; glass eyes; black fabric nose; no paw pads; f.j.; e.s. Rare size.
CONDITION: Good   PRICE: $475-up
(Right) Circa 1907. 12in (31cm); honey-colored mohair; shoe-button eyes; f.j.; e.s.
CONDITION: Good   PRICE: $750-up
Courtesy Donna Harrison-West.

Clown Bear. Circa 1929. 14in (36cm); white, blue and pink mohair; glass eyes; f.j.; e.s. Hat and ruff not original.
CONDITION: Good   PRICE: $400-up
Courtesy Sydney R. Charles.

(Left) Bear with Movable Eyes. Circa 1925; 16in (41cm); honey-colored mohair; celluloid movable googly-type eyes; pink felt paw pads; f.j.; e.s. CONDITION: Excellent   PRICE: $800-up (Center back) Bear with Movable Eyes. Circa 1930. 28in (71cm); short brown chenille plush; celluloid movable googly-type eyes; f.j.; e.s. CONDITION: Excellent   PRICE: $700-up (Right) Bear with Sleep Eyes. Circa 1925. 13in (33cm); gold-mohair; celluloid sleep eyes; f.j.; e.s. Overalls not original. CONDITION: Excellent   PRICE: $900-up *Courtesy Sherryl Shirran.*

Circa 1938. 22in (56cm); red, white and blue plush; large oval-shaped metal eyes; n.j.; s.s. CONDITION: Excellent   PRICE: $75-up *Courtesy Janice Penny.*

(Left) Teddy-Doll (Eskimo Doll). Circa 1910. 18in (46cm); brown wool plush; bisque face; glass sleep eyes; pin-jointed arms and legs; stationary head; beige felt hands and feet; e.s. CONDITION: Excellent   PRICE: $350-up (Right) Teddy Doll (Eskimo Doll). Circa 1910. 8in (20cm); bright red mohair; celluloid face; painted features; f.j.; e.s. CONDITION: Excellent   PRICE: $150-up *Courtesy Patricia Volpe.*

Unmarked American Manufactured Bears and Animals

Circa 1930. 19in (48cm); bright gold mohair; short gold mohair in-set snout; glass eyes (set wide apart); f.j.; e.s.
CONDITION: Excellent
PRICE: $250-up
Courtesy Lillian Rohaly

(Left) Possibly E.I. Horsman. *Chantecler Doll.* Circa 1912. 14in (36cm); celluloid doll face; painted features; green, orange and brown felt feathers; short pale gold mohair body; jointed pale gold velveteen legs; swivel head; e.s. The Chantecler is a character in an old fairy tale. Rare.

CONDITION: Excellent   **PRICE:** $600-up
(Right) Teddy Doll. Circa 1908. 13in (33cm); short vivid purple mohair; celluloid face; painted features; f.j.; e.s.; beige felt hands and feet. Teddy Dolls are also referred to as Eskimo Dolls.
CONDITION: Good   **PRICE:** $300-up

Possibly Ideal. Circa 1908. 20in (51cm);
gold mohair; shoe-button eyes; f.j.; e.s.
(stuffed hard).
CONDITION: Excellent
PRICE: $1100-up
Courtesy Barbara Baldwin

Possums

The toy industry jumped on the "possum bandwagon" when President William H. Taft adopted the creature as a mascot. Billy Possum could never compete with the teddy bear.

Today, Billy Possum toys and related memorabilia are extremely rare and desirable collector's items.

(Left) Circa 1909. 11in (28cm) long gray mohair; shoe-button eyes; f.j.; beige felt tail; brown felt ears; e.s.
CONDITION: Excellent
PRICE: $800-up
(Center) Circa 1909. 11in (28cm); long white mohair; blue faded stripes; shoe-button eyes; f.j.; beige felt tail and ears; e.s.
CONDITION: Excellent
PRICE: $650-up

(Left) **H. Fisher and Co.** Billy Possum. Circa 1909. 9in (23cm); gray mohair; gray felt ears and tail; f.j.; swivel tail; e.s. H. Fisher and Company manufactured the first version of Billy Possum in 1909.
CONDITION: Excellent   **PRICE:** $650-up
(Center) **Steiff** Possum. Circa 1909. 12in (31cm); silky beige mohair; short beige mohair inset snout; gray felt tail; brown felt ears; airbrushed features; rust-colored pearl cotton nose, mouth and claws; shoe-button eyes; f.j. swivel (wired) tail; e.s.; <u>FF</u> button; trace white S.L. Rare. Steiff quickly responded to the new American toy by producing their version of an opossum in three sizes from 1909 until 1914.
CONDITION: Excellent   **PRICE:** $3500-up
(Right) ***Billy Possum.*** Circa 1909. 9½in (25cm); gray mohair; glass eyes; f.j.; swivel tail; e.s.
CONDITION: Excellent   **PRICE:** $400-up
Courtesy Barbara Lauver.

See also Steiff Animals, pages 117 and 118.

CHAPTER 2
BRITISH BEARS AND SOFT TOYS

Chad Valley

Dating back to the mid-nineteenth century as a lithographic printing and stationery house, Chad Valley first came on the scene as a teddy bear manufacturer in 1915. Its first bear came in 13 different sizes and was made with five different furs. During the years of the first World War, no trademark restrictions were enforced, so Chad Valley bears sported metal buttons in their ears, mimicking their Steiff cousins in Germany. This identifying mark first emerged around 1920 as a metal ring around a blue paper disk, covered by cellophane. By the 1930s, the button was a typical sheet metal format with a blue outer ring and a yellow paper inside with the words "Chad Valley English Hygienic Toys." Prior to the 1930s, Chad Valley bears were also identified with an oblong label on the foot. When Queen Elizabeth appointed Chad Valley as Royal toy makers (1938), a Royal Crest on a square was stitched to the bear's foot.

Characteristics of Chad Valley bears include a wide stitched nose and vibrant mohair colors.

(Top) Circa 1930. A clear celluloid covers a metal button with the words "CHAD VALLEY BRITISH HYGIENIC TOYS." This button was affixed to the ear on a majority of Chad Valley's early products.

(Center) Circa 1930. Chad Valley used a "woven" label (usually sewn on the foot) in addition to the button.

(Bottom) 1938 to 1960s. Chad Valley was granted their Royal Warrant of Appointment as Toymakers to Her Majesty the Queen (now Queen Elizabeth, the Queen Mother) in 1938. The label (usually a square label stitched to the foot) depicted the Royal Crest.

Circa 1930. 12in (31cm); red mohair; glass eyes; f.j.; e.s. Metal button covered with clear plastic affixed to ear reads: "CHAD VALLEY/BRITISH HYGIENIC TOYS." Rare color.
CONDITION: Excellent
PRICE: $750-up
Courtesy Dottie Ayers.

BELOW:
(Left) Circa 1930. 22in (56cm); gold mohair; glass eyes; f.j.; excelsior and kapok stuffing; label sewn into side seam reads: "Hygienic Toy/Made in England/Chad Valley/Chiltern."
CONDITION: Fair
PRICE: $500-up
(Right) Circa 1960. 12in (31cm); gold mohair; glass eyes; f.j.; excelsior and kapok stuffing; label sewn onto foot reads: "The Chad Valley Co. Ltd. By Appointment Toy Makers to H.M. Queen Elizabeth The Queen Mother." It also pictures the family crest. Tag attached to bear reads: (front) "By Appointment with Queen Elizabeth the Queen Mother Toymaker." (Back) "Real Mohair Luxury Soft Toy/Chad Valley/Chiltern/Made in England."
CONDITION: Mint
PRICE: $525-up
Courtesy Suzanne Irvin and M.L. Campbell.

OPPOSITE PAGE:
(Left) Circa 1940. 20in (51cm); gold mohair; glass eyes; "wide" stitched nose; f.j.; k.s.
CONDITION: Excellent   **PRICE:** $550-up
(Right) Circa 1940. 15in (38cm); gold mohair; glass eyes; "wide" stitched nose; glass eyes; f.j.; k.s.
CONDITION: Excellent   **PRICE:** $450-up
Courtesy Ho Phi Le.

(Left) Circa 1950. 15in (38in); white wool; red rexine paw pads; glass eyes; f.j.; s.s.; square printed label stitched to foot reads:"By Appointment to H.M. Queen Elizabeth. Toymaker The Chad Valley Co. Ltd." Printed label stitched to side seam reads: "Hygienic Toys. Made in England. The Chad Valley Co."
CONDITION: Excellent   **PRICE:** $400-up
(Right) Circa 1930. 18in (46cm); blonde-colored mohair; glass eyes; f.j.; e.s. head; k.s. body; metal button covered with clear plastic affixed to ear reads: "CHAD VALLEY/BRITISH HYGIENIC TOYS." Woven label on foot reads: "Hygienic Toys/Made in England by Chad Valley Co., Ltd."
CONDITION: Excellent   **PRICE:** $625-up
Courtesy Jeanne A. Miller.

Toffee. Circa 1954. 10in (25cm); toffee-colored mohair; glass eyes; f.j.; excelsior and kapok stuffing. Label on foot reads: "By Appointment to H.M. Queen Elizabeth The Queen Mother/ Toymakers The Chad Valley Co. Ltd." Paper hang tag reads: "Toffee/The Teddy with a Personality/From the Broadcast Stories of 'Lulupet & Toffee' by Jane Alan."
CONDITION: Mint   **PRICE:** $300-up
Private collection.

"Sooty" Puppet - *See also **Unmarked British Manufacturers**, page 48.*

Chiltern

A German immigrant and a former employee of J.K. Farnell Co. joined together to create Chiltern Toy Works in 1908. Over the years, this British company was responsible for myriad of popular bears, animals and toys. Most notably were **Bruin**, acquired along with a range of soft toys called Panurge. Others had music boxes and voice boxes. *Chubby bears* were introduced in 1931. Soon after in that same year these bears were re-christened *Hugmee*.

Early *Hugmee Bears* had muzzles, broad smiles, embroidered claws and a large ribbon bow. In the 1950s, the mohair plush is less luxurious, the smile is gone, the bow smaller and less thread appears on the claws. Retaining the basic characteristics of the originals, these bears still are plumper with shorter legs than others manufactured by the plant. In 1960 plastic noses were tried, but the embroidery look prevailed.

(Right) Circa 1960. 21in (53cm); long honey-colored mohair; glass eyes; velveteen paw pads; foot pads reinforced with cardboard; f.j.; e.s. head; k.s. body.
CONDITION: Excellent   **PRICE: $450-up**
(Center) **Unmarked British manufacturer** (possibly Chad Valley). Circa 1930. 21in (53cm); short honey-colored mohair; glass eyes; f.j.; e.s. head; k.s. body.
CONDITION: Good   **PRICE: $400-up**
(Left) **Unidentified British manufacturer.** Circa 1930. 21in (54cm); long gold mohair; velveteen paw pads; glass eyes; f.j.; e.s. head; k.s. body.
CONDITION: Excellent   **PRICE: $425-up**
Courtesy Margaret and Gerry Grey.

Circa 1950. 21in (53cm); honey-colored mohair; glass eyes; velveteen paw pads; f.j.; k.s.
CONDITION: Excellent   **PRICE: $450-up**
Courtesy Sally Bowen.

Dean's Childplay Toys

The history of the oldest existing British toy manufacturer begins in 1903 when Dean's was a publisher of soft cloth books. By 1912, the company's "Rag Knock-about Toy Sheets" series produced puppets, toy animals and dolls in a soft woolly cloth. Identified by a logo of two fighting dogs, this popular company patented the concept of "evripose" joints which allowed animals to be moved into virtually every position. Bears on wheels were produced in 1920.

Other famous Dean creations were Felix the Cat, and for a brief time, Mickey Mouse (1930). Abandoning the fighting dog signature, the company continued the production of teddy bears as part of a much larger mix. However, after World War II, Dean's concentrated on making teddy bears, Golliwogs, animals and a variety of soft cuddly toys.

A woven and later printed label identified Dean's Rag Book soft toys. A metal button with the incised words "Dean's Rag Book Co. Ltd." was also affixed to their early products.

LEFT:
(Left) Circa 1930. 15in (38cm); honey-colored mohair; glass eyes; f.j.; e.s. head; k.s. body.
CONDITION: Excellent   PRICE: $550-up
(Center) *Dismal Desmond.* Circa 1923. 5in (13cm); white velveteen with black painted spots; painted facial features; n.j.; k.s. Manufacturer's trademark of two dogs fiercely tugging on one of the Dean's Rag Books is printed around neck. Also printed around neck: "MADE IN ENGLAND/DISMAL DESMOND/BY DEAN'S RAG BOOK COMPANY."
CONDITION: Good   PRICE: $100-up
(Right) Circa 1930. 12in (31cm); pale gold-colored mohair; glass eyes; f.j.; e.s. head; k.s. body. Label stitched to foot reads: "MADE IN ENGLAND BY DEAN'S RAG BOOK CO., LTD., LONDON."
CONDITION: Excellent   PRICE: $475-up

Mickey Mouse Triketoy. Circa 1930. 12in (31cm); black and beige velveteen; celluloid disc googly eyes; flexible (unjointed) body; stationary head; s.s. Mickey is attached to a metal tricycle giving the appearance Mickey is pedaling when toy is drawn along by a string.
CONDITION: Good
PRICE: Sold at Sotheby's May 1990 Auction for £715 (approximately $1500).
Courtesy Sotheby's.

See also page 47.

J.K. Farnell

A white woven label was attached to the foot of the early J.K. Farnell teddy bears.

Certainly one of the oldest soft toy manufacturers in the world, this British company is closely linked with the earliest origins of the teddy bear. Founded by Agnes Farnell in 1840, the company claims that its turn-of-the-century creations even influenced Margarete Steiff's entree into the world of teddy bears. This pioneer toy manufacturer is known for its extensive line of dolls, animals and, especially teddy bears. The prototype of Winnie-the-Pooh is said to be a Farnell bear.

Although highly-regarded for their high quality, Farnell bears were machine-seamed. Hand-embroidery on the face, nose and paws assured individuality. The faces on early designs are very appealing. Early body characteristics are long curved arms, long legs and large feet. A percentage have webbed stitched paw designs. Their mohair is mainly long and silky. The company continued producing until the early 1960s.

Circa 1930. 28in (71cm); white mohair; glass eyes; brown stitched nose and mouth; f.j.; e.s. head; k.s. body.
CONDITION: Good
PRICE: $1300-up

Circa 1960. 16in (41cm); gold mohair; plastic eyes; f.j.; e.s. snout; k.s. head and body. Label sewn into chest reads: "This is a Farnell Quality Soft Toy/Made in Hastings, England."
CONDITION: Good   PRICE: $250-up
Courtesy Susan Engebretson.

Circa 1936. 27in (68cm); long silky gold mohair; glass eyes; f.j.; k.s. body; e.s. head; rexine paw pads. Label stitched to foot reads: "A Farnell Alpha Toy/Made in England."
CONDITION: Mint   PRICE: $1500-up
Courtesy Gale Darter.

Gabrielle Designs Ltd.
(Left) *Paddington Bear.* Circa 1980. 19in (48cm); beige acrylic plush; plastic eyes; black plastic nose; f.j.; s.s. Label sewn into seam at back reads: "Gabrielle Designs Ltd./Made in England." C.T. reads: "Darkest Peru/To London, England via Paddington Stn." Reverse of tag reads: "Please look after this bear. Thank you." Dressed in gray felt duffle coat, blue felt hat and blue rubber boots.
CONDITION: Excellent
PRICE: $75-up

(Right) *Aunt Lucy.* Circa 1978; 18in (46cm); grayish brown-colored acrylic plush; plastic eyes; plastic nose; f.j.; s.s.; label sewn into seam at back reads: "This bear is protected by copyright 1978/Gabrielle Designs Ltd/Doncaster U.K./U.K. Desig." The reverse of the manufacturer's chest tag reads: "Aunt Lucy/c/o The Home for Retired Bears/Lima/Peru." Dressed in a red and white printed skirt, black and white checked shawl, red scarf, black felt hat and shoes and plastic glasses.
CONDITION: Excellent
PRICE: $75-up

House of Nisbet

(Left) *Aloysious Bear.* 1986. 23in (58cm); gold-colored "distressed" mohair; plastic eyes; f.j.; s.s. Comes with British Airways bag. First version. Limited edition 2500 world wide.
CONDITION: Mint
PRICE: $250-up
(Right) *Aloysious Bear.* 1986. 13½in (34cm); gold mohair; plastic eyes; f.j.; s.s. Comes with British Airways sack. Second version. Limited edition 5000 world wide.
CONDITION: Mint
PRICE: $150-up
Courtesy Jerry and Bill Elliott.

Merrythought

Merrythought, an old English term for wishbone began as a small spinning mill in 1919. It was not until 1930 that Merrythought Toys opened with personnel from Chad Valley and J.K. Farnell. Although Merrythought has produced many different products, fortunately for the collector the company maintained good identification of its toys over the years.

Even though realistic animals and dolls (the earliest being the Golliwog) were produced, it is the traditional teddy bear that was Merrythought's line from the onset.

These highly collectible creations were fully jointed, made of high quality mohair or "art silk plush." Brown glass eyes and kapok stuffing are further identifying materials. Certain Merrythought bears are known by their unusual design of webbed paw stitching and a wide vertically stitched nose.

(Top) 1935-1939. Merrythought affixed a button to their bears and animals in the ear and later on the back of the body. Clear celluloid covers the metal button showing the Merrythought trademark, a wishbone with the words: "Regd trademark HYGIENIC MERRYTHOUGHT TOYS/MADE IN ENGLAND."
(Center) 1931-1947. Merrythought used a "woven" label (usually sewn on the foot) in addition to the button. Later, the label was used on its own.
(Bottom) 1947-1990. A "printed" label (usually sewn on the foot) identified the Merrythought bears or animals. Note the information has changed from the woven label. Currently Merrythought is using an embroidered label on all their products.

Circa 1930. 18in (46cm); silky gold mohair; glass eyes; f.j.; e.s. head; k.s. body. Clear celluloid covered metal button in left ear reads: "Regd. Trademark Hygienic Merrythought Toys/ Made in England." Woven label on foot reads: "Merrythought Hygienic Toys/Made in England."
CONDITION: Mint
PRICE: $800-up
Courtesy Ian Pout.

BELOW:
(Left) Circa 1930. 18in (46cm); blonde mohair; glass eyes; f.j.; e.s. head; k.s. body. Clear celluloid metal button in left ear reads: "Regd Trademark Hygienic Merrythought Toys/Made in England." Woven label on foot reads: "MERRYTHOUGHT TOYS/MADE IN ENGLAND."
CONDITION: Fair
PRICE: $450-up
(Right) *Nightdress Case Bear.* Circa 1950. 23in (58m); gold mohair; glass eyes; f.j.; k.s. head. Printed label on foot reads: "MERRYTHOUGHT IRONBRIDGE, SHROPS/MADE IN ENGLAND."
CONDITION: Excellent
PRICE: $300-up

(Left) *Cheeky Bear.* Circa 1955. 10in (25cm); bright gold mohair; gold velveteen in-set snout; brown felt pads; glass eyes; f.j.; k.s.; bell in ear.
CONDITION: Mint   **PRICE:** $125-up
(Right) *Cheeky Bear.* Circa 1955. 15in (38cm); bright gold mohair; gold velveteen in-set snout; brown felt pads; glass eyes; f.j.; k.s.; bell in ear.
CONDITION: Mint   **PRICE:** $175-up

Punkinhead Bear. Circa 1952. 22in (56cm); brown and gold mohair; velveteen in-set snout and tops of feet; glass eyes; f.j.; e.s. Rare size.
CONDITION: Excellent   **PRICE:** $500-up
Courtesy Geri Evans.

Omega

Omega. Circa 1914. 11in (28cm) tall by 12in (31cm) long; dark brown mohair; glass eyes (color painted on back); f.j.; e.s.; marks on wooden wheels read: "British Made J.R." Bear is mounted on metal frame. As toy is pulled, bear moves back and forth. Note resemblance to Steiff's Record Teddy (page 84)..
CONDITION: Excellent
PRICE: $1000-up

Wendy Boston Soft Toys

Although not very well known, this firm claims to have made 28% of all soft toys exported from Britain in the 1960s. It also claims to have made the very first nylon teddy bear around 1955.

This prolific designer produced numerous soft and cuddly teddy bears which can easily be identified by their large round heads, close cropped snouts, small triangular wedged shaped embroidered noses, and large fixed outstretched arms and legs. A mohair jointed teddy was also made in the more traditional manner.

The House of Nisbet currently owns the Wendy Boston name.

(Left) Golliwog. Circa 1950. 19in (48cm); black cotton fabric face, hands and legs; painted facial features; red corduroy jacket and shoes (an integral part of body); striped cotton skirt; black synthetic hair; s.s. manufacturer's silk label sewn onto foot.
CONDITION: Excellent   PRICE: $200-up
(Center) Circa 1960. 16in (41cm); beige synthetic nylon plush; plastic eyes; n.j.; foam chip stuffing. Manufacturer's silk label sewn into side seam of bear.
CONDITION: Excellent   PRICE: $175-up
(Right) Panda. Circa 1960. 9in (22cm); black and white synthetic nylon plush; plastic eyes; n.j.; s.s. Manufacturer's silk label sewn into back seam.
CONDITION: Excellent   PRICE: $100-up
Courtesy Margaret and Gerry Grey.

Unidentified British Manufactured Bears and Animals

Circa 1920. 25in (64cm); light gold mohair; glass eyes; f.j.; e.s.
CONDITION: Excellent
PRICE: $1200-up
Private collection.

Circa 1940. 34in (86cm); gold mohair; glass eyes; f.j.; e.s. head; k.s. body; rexine paw pads.
CONDITION: Excellent
PRICE: $500-up
Courtesy Elsa B. Malcolm.

ABOVE:
(Left) Sooty-type Bear. Circa 1960. 10in (25cm); gold and black cotton plush; plastic eyes; f.j.; e.s.
CONDITION: Excellent
PRICE: $150-up
(Center) **Dean's Rag Book Company.** Circa 1950. 15in (38cm); pale gold-colored mohair; short mohair in-set snout; glass eyes; velveteen paw pads; f.j.; s.s.; Dean's label sewn into side seam.
CONDITION: Excellent
PRICE: $250-up
(Right) Panda. Circa 1960. 12in (31cm); black and white mohair; glass eyes; f.j.; s.s.
CONDITION: Excellent
PRICE: $150-up
Courtesy The Rare Bear.

Felix the Cat. Circa 1920. 25¼in (64cm); short black mohair; short white mohair in-set snout; wide toothey grin; f.j.; e.s. Felix holds a photograph of his original owners posing at the seaside with a life-size model of himself.
CONDITION: Excellent
PRICE: Sold at Sotheby's May 1990 Auction for £660 (approximately $1190).
Courtesy Sotheby's.

Unmarked British Manufactured Bears

Possibly J.K. Farnell. Circa 1915. 16in (41cm); blonde-colored mohair; shoe-button eyes; f.j.; webbed stitched paws; e.s.
CONDITION: Excellent
PRICE: $1600-up
Courtesy Patricia Volpe.

(Left) Probably Twyford. Circa 1940. 15in (38cm); white mohair; glass eyes; tan stitched nose, mouth and claws; beige rexine paw pads; f.j.; e.s. head; k.s. body.
CONDITION: Excellent   **PRICE:** $250-up
(Center) **Chad Valley** *Sooty Puppet.* Circa 1960. 9in (23cm); gold mohair; plastic eyes; jointed head; e.s. head.
CONDITION: Good   **PRICE:** $55-up
(Right) Probably Chiltern. Musical Bear. Circa 1950. 18in (46cm); blonde silky mohair; glass eyes; f.j.; e.s. head; k s. body; velveteen paw pads. A small cylinder-type music box is encased in bellows concealed in the tummy. Music is produced by squeezing bellows.
CONDITION: Excellent   **PRICE:** $400-up

Possibly Twyford. Circa 1935. 25in (63cm); gold mohair; red rexine paw pads; glass eyes; f.j.; e.s. body and head; k.s. arms and legs.
CONDITION: Excellent   **PRICE:** $300
Courtesy Sue Geary.

CHAPTER 3
GERMAN BEARS AND SOFT TOYS
Gebrüder Bing

Founded in 1865 as a tin and kitchenware company, Gebrüder Bing is most known for its fine clockwork bears and toys of the early twentieth century.

Walking, climbing and tumbling bears made by Bing are prized collector's items today. Mainly covered in short beige or brown mohair, many of the Bing bears were dressed in colorful felt and silk outfits.

It is extremely rare to find a Bing bear with its original small metal tag affixed to the edge of the ear with the letters "G.B.N." (Gebrüder Bing Nürnberg) in the center of a diamond design. Sometimes on its own or along with the tag, an orange or white painted metal button was securely fastened under the arm on the bear's body. The "G.B.N." mark was used until 1919 when it was replaced by "B.W." (Bing Werke) in 1920.

The 1920s non-mechanical bears from Bing have a much longer snout than their earlier counterparts. They also have long curly mohair and glass eyes. It appears the "B.W." (Bing Werke) metal tag was then affixed to the lower arm.

(Left) Circa 1910. 14in (36cm); white mohair; rust-colored pearl cotton stitched nose, mouth and claws; shoe-button eyes; f.j.; e.s.; metal tag fastened to right ear with the letters G.B.N. (Gebrüder Bing Nürnberg) in the center of a diamond design. Magnificent example of early Bing teddy bear in mint condition. Especially rare with early identification tag. Note the similarity to Steiff bears from the same era.
CONDITION: Mint   PRICE: $5000-up
(Right) Circa 1910. 10in (25cm); gold mohair; shoe-button eyes; f.j.; e.s.; metal button fastened to left side of body (just visible in illustration) with the letters G.B.N. (Gebrüder Bing Nürnberg) in the center of a diamond design. Note arms and body are "plumper" compared to a Steiff bear's body in this size and same era.
CONDITION: Mint   PRICE: $2000-up
Private collection.

Mechanical Bear. Circa 1908. 20in (51cm); gray mohair; shoe-button eyes; f.j.; e.s.; metal disk at neck joint. When key (located at side of body) is wound, head turns from side to side.
CONDITION: Excellent   PRICE: $6000-up

Tumbling Acro Bear. Circa 1910. 13in (33cm); short cinnamon-colored mohair; shoe-button eyes; f.j.; e.s.; metal button affixed to side of body. Arms wind clockwork mechanism to activate tumbling motion. Metal hooks are attached to end of paws to enable bear to be hung while in tumbling motion.
CONDITION: Excellent   **PRICE:** $4500-up
Private collection.

Mechanical Bears. Circa 1912. (Left) 6½in (16cm); (Right) 8in (20cm); short cinnamon-colored mohair; shoe-button eyes; jointed arms and legs; stationary head; e.s. (firmly stuffed). When wound with key, bears push brightly painted metal balls (left [painted red]); (right [painted blue]) with white stars that support the bear's right arm. The clockwork mechanism is concealed in ball that causes them to move. Rare.
CONDITION: Excellen
PRICE: (Left) $4000-up
          (Right) $4500-up
Private collection.

(Left) Roller-Skating Bear. Circa 1912. 8in (20cm); short dark brown mohair; shoe-button eyes; f.j.; e.s.; dressed in felt jacket and cotton pants. Body encases key wind mechanism. Action: With the aid of an attached walking stick, set to move up and down, the bear leans back and forth as it travels forward.
CONDITION: Excellent   **PRICE:** $4500-up
(Right) Roller-Skating Bear. Circa 1912. 8in (20cm); short beige mohair; shoe-button eyes; f.j.; e.s.; metal button fastened to side of body reads: "DRP DIV, DRGM." Same mechanism and action as bear on left.
CONDITION: Excellent   **PRICE:** $4000-up
Private collection.

Circa 1915. 25in (64 cm); long silky gold mohair; shoe-button eyes; f.j.; e.s.; round metal button with a trace of orange paint is affixed to side of body. Wide head and small ears denote this bear to be Bing.
CONDITION: Excellent
PRICE: $5000-up
Private collection.

Circa 1919. 19in (48cm); pale beige mohair; glass eyes (color painted on back); f.j.; e.s.
CONDITION: Good   **PRICE:** $1500-up
Courtesy Denise Grey.

Circa 1920. 26in (66cm); honey-colored mohair; orange-colored (painted on back) glass eyes; f.j.; e.s.
CONDITION: Excellent   **PRICE:** $4200-up
Courtesy Barbara Baldwin.

Circa 1920. 20in (51cm); bright cinnamon-col-
ored mohair; bright orange glass eyes; f.j.; e.s.
CONDITION: Excellent   PRICE: $3500-up
Private collection.

Clemens

The Clemens family first used old woolen army blankets to produce a lovable teddy bear for German children to hold and cuddle following World War II. Their success soon led them to manufacture other soft toys and today the firm makes thousands of toys a month.

Circa 1940. 17in (43cm); cinnamon-mohair; glass eyes; f.j.; e.s.
CONDITION: Fair
PRICE: $250-up
Courtesy Volker Schneider.

Circa 1950. 16in (41cm); beige mohair; short mohair in-set snout; glass eyes; f.j.; e.s.; metal tag reads: "Clemens/West Germany." Without the company's tag this Clemens design could be confused with a Hermann bear.
CONDITION: Excellent
PRICE: $200-up
Courtesy Lillian Rohaly.

Eduard Crämer

Bearkin Bear. Circa 1930. 11in (28cm); golden brown-colored mohair; short mohair heart-shaped face; glass eyes; f.j.; s.s.; original trousseau; clothes and accessories marked "Germany." Rare.
CONDITION: Excellent
PRICE: $1500-up
Courtesy Barbara Baldwin.

(Left) Circa 1930; 27in (69cm); long white silky mohair; open mouth lined with pink felt; pink felt tongue; brown pearl cotton stitched nose, mouth and claws; glass eyes; f.j.; e.s.
CONDITION: Excellent
PRICE: $4000-up
(Right) Circa 1930. 22in (56cm); long white silky mohair; open mouth lined with pink felt; sculptured pink felt tongue; glass eyes; f.j.; e.s. Note short mohair heart-shaped face denotes one of this company's traits.
CONDITION: Excellent
PRICE: $3500-up
Courtesy Barbara Lauver (bear on left) and Deborah Ratliff (bear on right).

Grisly

Grisly® bears have not changed much since their inception in 1954, when Karl Unfrecht founded the company of Grisly Spielwaren Fabrik. When he died in 1980, his children, Hans-Georg Unfrecht and Hannelore Wirth, took over the company.

Originally, the company identified their products with a metal button fastened to the chest of the animal. Their trademark was a needle and thread super-imposed upon a standing bear. The name Grisly® is also printed on the button. Due to the expense, the button was discontinued in 1984 and a tag with the same logo is now attached to the animal. One distinct feature of their bears is an oversized head.

Circa 1960. 22in (56cm); beige mohair; glass eyes; f.j.; k.s.; paper tag attached to chest reads: "Grisly/Made in Western Germany." This disproportionately large head and in-set snout are characteristic of Grisly®.
CONDITION: Mint   PRICE: $325-up
Courtesy Kay and Wayne Jensen.

(Front row) Circa 1992. 10in (25cm); vivid green mohair; (left front) bright red mohair (right front) green mohair; beige in-set snouts and paw pads; plastic eyes; f.j.; s.s.
CONDITION: Mint
PRICE: $45-up
(Center row left) Bear on wheels. Circa 1992. 10in (25cm) by 5in (13cm); dark brown mohair; beige mohair in-set snout; plastic eyes; n.j.; s.s.
CONDITION: Mint
PRICE: $75-up
(Center row center) Circa 1991. 7in (18cm); pale gold mohair; short gold mohair in-set snout and paw pads; plastic eyes; f.j.; s.s.
CONDITION: Mint   PRICE: $32-up
(Center right) Bear On All Fours. Circa 1991. 10in (25cm) by 5in (13cm); beige mohair; plastic eyes; n.j.; s.s.
CONDITION: Mint   PRICE: $40-up

(Center back) Circa 1991. 28in (71cm); caramel-tipped with white mohair; short beige mohair in-set snout paw pads and lining of ears; f.j.; e.s.
CONDITION: Mint   PRICE: $325-up
Courtesy The Bear Bare Co. Inc.

Hermann

Circa 1940. 24in (61cm); long silky cream-colored mohair; short mohair in-set snout; brown stitched nose, mouth and claws; glass eyes; f.j.; e.s.
CONDITION: Good   PRICE: $500-up
Courtesy Volker Schneider.

Hermann is one of the oldest family-owned teddy bear manufacturers in Germany, originall founded by Johann Hermann, a native of a smal village near Sonneberg, the toy capital of the world. Bernard Hermann, Johann's oldest son founded the Gebrüder Hermann K.G. (Hermann Brothers Company) in 1911, and for the first time bears produced by this company bore their trade mark "BE-HA.", an abbreviation of his first and last names. Bernard had four sons. One, Mr Werner Hermann was the sole designer of all Gebrüder Hermann teddy bears. Since 1987, hi niece Mrs. Trautl Mischner-Hermann has joined him in designing the line. His late brother Arthu was the business manager of the present Gebrüde Hermann Company.

The other Hermann who became famous in the teddy bear world is Max Hermann. In 1920, he founded his own plush animal and teddy bea company. Today, his son Rolf, the president of the Hermann Spielwaren GmbH, produces a line o plush bears and animals. "The bear with the running dog" and the green triangle continue to be their trademark.

There are two more Hermanns of note. Mrs Ida Hermann, a sister of Bernard and Max Hermann, married into a Bavarian family called the Baumann family, known today as the "Baki" Company. They mostly produce teddy bears made of inexpensive material used as carnival prizes.

The last member of the Johann Hermann clan is Mr. Arthur Hermann, the youngest son of the Hermann family. In 1913, Mr. Arthur Hermann founded the Hermann Toy Company. As a trademark he had an upright walking teddy bear pulling a teddy bear on wheels and a little monkey as the passenger. Later the trademark changed to a crown with capital letters REX, and it was a registered trademark until 1954 when Arthur died, and the company ceased to exist.

Gebrüder Hermann K.G. (Left) Circa 1950 12in (31cm); gold mohair; "three" claws on paws and feet; glass eyes; f.j.; e.s.
CONDITION: Good   PRICE: $250-up
(Center) Circa 1930. 18in (46cm); long silky gold mohair; short mohair in-set snout; "three" claws on paws and feet; no side seams in body; glass eyes; f.j.; e.s.
CONDITION: Excellent   PRICE: $400-up
(Right) Circa 1950. 19in (48cm); beige mohair; short beige mohair in-set snout; glass eyes; f.j.; e.s.
CONDITION: Excellent   PRICE: $300-up

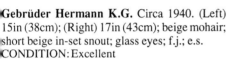

Gebrüder Hermann K.G. Circa 1940. (Left) 15in (38cm); (Right) 17in (43cm); beige mohair; short beige in-set snout; glass eyes; f.j.; e.s. CONDITION: Excellent
PRICE: 15in (38cm) $300
17in (43cm) $325
Courtesy Sally Bowen.

Gebrüder Hermann K.G. *Rose Bear.* (Tea Party Series.) 1992. 6½in (16cm); pink mohair; plastic eyes; f.j.; s.s. Dressed in a velvet rose-colored dress with rose at ear. Limited edition of 2000.
CONDITION: Mint   **PRICE:** $120-up
Courtesy Kathy Ann Doll Imports, Inc.

Gebrüder Hermann K.G. *German Wall Bear.* 1990. 12in (31cm); honey gold-colored mohair; short mohair in-set snout; felt lined open mouth; glass eyes; f.j.; s.s. A piece of rock that he carries in the bag was taken from the wall that separated East from West Germany. Limited edition of 1000 for the American market and 1000 for the European market. Designed by Edna Smith.
CONDITION: Mint
PRICE: $150-up
Courtesy Edna Smith.

Hermann Spielwaren GmbH. Circa 1950. 20in (51cm); dark brown mohair; short beige mohair in-set snout; "three" claws on paws and feet; no side seams in body; glass eyes; f.j.; e.s.; gold and green metallic tag attached to bear's chest reads: "Hermann Pluschtiere/Made in Germany." Also pictured on the tag is a bear with the running dog. CONDITION: Mint   **PRICE:** $250-up

Gebrüder Sussenguth

Gebrüder Sussenguth. Peter Bears. Circa 1925. (Left) 14in (36cm); dark gray mohair tipped in white. (Center) 17in (43cm); apricot-colored mohair. (Right) 14in (36cm); blonde mohair tipped in dark brown. All bears have googly glass eyes; open mouth; carved wooden teeth and tongue; f.j.; e.s.; chest tag reads: "Peter ges. gesh (legally protected) #895257." When head is turned, eyes and tongue move from side to side. Note: A wooden-eyed version was also produced in the blonde mohair tipped in dark brown. Prices are slightly less than the glass-eyed version. CONDITION: Mint
PRICE: (Left) $3000-up
              (Center) $5000-up
              (Right) $2800-up
Private collection.

Petz

The Petz Company was located in Neustadt and, until 1974, made a large variety of the old nostalgic style of teddy bears. Mohair Petz bears measured up to 40in(101cm), and the Petz Company produced between 12,000 to 14,000 bears a year in their prime.

Circa 1935. 22in (56cm); deep cinnamon-colored mohair; glass eyes; f.j.; e.s.; milk glass button with "Petz" incised in red affixed to chest.
CONDITION: Excellent
PRICE: $850-up
Courtesy Sydney R. Charles.

Circa 1940. 19in (48cm); gold mohair tipped with reddish-brown; short blonde mohair in-set snout; glass eyes; f.j.; e.s. Milk glass button fastened to chest with the word "PETZ" embossed in red. Label sewn into seam of arm reads: "Original PETZ." Made in Germany.
CONDITION: Excellent
PRICE: $650-up
Private collection.

Kersa

The German company Kersa was
founded in 1925. Until 1960 they produced jointed teddy bears and animals
of plush. Since 1960 they changed
their line of merchandise and now
produce hand-puppets with cloth and
carved wooden heads. Early Kersa
animals were identified with a metal
tag affixed to the ear, later the metal
tag was affixed to sole of shoe.

Rabbit. Circa 1930. 11in (28cm); white
wool plush head and feet (airbrushed
in brown); felt body and hands; glass
eyes; unjointed arms and legs; swivel
head; e.s.; metal tag affixed to ear
reads: "KERSA"; brown felt coat; tan
plaid felt pants; celluloid glasses.
CONDITION: Excellent
PRICE: $350-up
Private collection.

Rabbits. Circa 1960. (Left) 5in (13cm);
(Right) 9in (23cm); tan felt heads and
bodies; black button eyes; jointed arms;
stationary legs and head; e.s. Dressed
in felt and cotton clothes. Metal tag
affixed to base of shoe reads:
"KERSA."
CONDITION: Mint
PRICE: (Left) $150-up
            (Right) $200-up
Private collection.

Schuco Toy Company

Yes/No Bear. Circa 1926. 14in (36cm); short bright blue mohair; shoe-button eyes; f.j.; e.s.
Head nods "yes" or "no" when tail is moved. Very rare color.
CONDITION: Mint   **PRICE:** $4500-up
Courtesy Barbara Baldwin.

Schuco Toy Company

After learning the toy business at Gebrüder Bing, Heinrich Muller combined forces with Heinrich Schreyer and formed Schuco in 1912. It survived Hitler and World War II, but eventually it could not compete with the Japanese toy industry. After fifty years, Schuco (an abbreviation for Schreyer and Co.) closed its doors, leaving behind a toy legacy of collectibles still highly prized the world over.

Originally noted for its mechanical toys, Schuco bears and animals delighted children by somersaulting and walking.

Dressed in non-removable outfits, Schuco bears came primarily in short bristle-type mohair and vibrant colors.

Sometimes compacts and perfume bottles were concealed in miniature bears. Other times, these little creatures drove key-wound cars and scooters.

Schuco received the most recognition for its "yes/no" mechanism which worked by moving the tail to direct the animal's head in any direction. The most popular of this genre is now known as "The Bellhop" unveiled in 1926.

Early Schuco mechanical bears are closely aligned in design to those of Gebrüder Bing with small facial features, head, ears, slightly upturned snout, slim body, narrow straight arms with slightly curved paws, round small feet and shiny shoe-button eyes, the non-mechanical Schuco bears have noticeably different identifying characteristics. The head is wide and ears quite large. The eyes are deep set, close together and very often made of clear glass. The mohair on these beautiful bears is long and silky. A later feature was the shearing of the muzzle and paw pads.

Yes/No Bell Hop Bear. Circa 1920. Short gold mohair head, paws and feet; glass eyes; red felt jacket and hat; black felt pants (clothes an integral part of body); f.j.; e.s. Head nods "yes" or "no" when tail is moved.
CONDITION: Excellent
PRICE: 8in (20cm) $2500-up
        12in (31cm) $3000-up
        17in (43cm) $4000-up
        20in (51cm) $5000-up

(Right) Circa 1920. 2⅜in (6cm) short white mohair covers metal head and body; black metal eyes; brown stitched nose and mouth; beige felt paws; f.j. Rare size, color and with felt paws. CONDITION: Mint **PRICE:** $350-up
(Center right) Circa 1920. 2⅜in (6cm); short brown mohair covers metal head and body; black metal eyes; f.j.
CONDITION: Excellent **PRICE:** $125-up

(Center left front and back) Monkeys. Circa 1920. 3½in (9cm); various vivid colors of mohair and felt cover metal frame; f.j.; beige felt paw pads. CONDITION: Excellent **PRICE:** $150-up
(Left) Monkey (Compact). 3½in (9cm); short lavender mohair covers metal frame; f.j. Removing head discloses compact. Rare color.
CONDITION: Excellent **PRICE:** $300-up

(Left) Bear (Compact). Circa 1920. 3½in (9cm); short lavender mohair covers metal head and body; black metal eyes; f.j. Removing head discloses compact. Rare.
CONDITION: Excellent **PRICE:** $850-up
(Center left and center) *Janus* (Two Faces). Circa 1950; 3½in (9cm); short brown and gold mohair covers metal heads and bodies; black metal eyes; f.j. Twisting brass knob at base of body changes faces. [Center left] bear's face; [Center] laughing face with an exposed tongue and black and white squinting eyes.

CONDITION: Mint **PRICE:** $600-up
(Center right) Bear (Compact). Circa 1920. 3½in (9cm); short red mohair covers metal head and body; black metal eyes; f.j. Removing head discloses compact. Rare, especially this color.
CONDITION: Excellent **PRICE:** $900-up
(Right) Bear (Perfume). Circa 1920. 3½in (9cm); short gold mohair covers metal head and body; black metal eyes; f.j. Removing head discloses perfume bottle.
CONDITION: Excellent **PRICE:** $400-up

(Left) Bear in Car. Circa 1927. 3½in (9cm) (Bear); short gold mohair covers metal body; black metal eyes; f.j. Bear is seated in painted metal car. Schuco's emblem is stamped on side of car.
CONDITION: Good
PRICE: $2000-up
(Right) Bear in Car. Circa 1927. 3½in (9cm) (Bear); short pink mohair (rare color) covers metal body; black metal eyes; f.j. Bear rides in painted metal car. Schuco's emblem is stamped on side of car.
CONDITION: Good
PRICE: $2500-up
Private collection.

LEFT:
Bear (Perfume Bottle). Circa 1920. 5in (13cm); "long" off-white mohair covers metal body; glass "sparkling" (faceted) eyes; f.j. Removal of head discloses glass perfume bottle.
CONDITION: Excellent
PRICE: $1000-up
Private collection.

(Left to right) Yes/No Bell Hop. Circa 1923. 9½in (24cm); short gold mohair head and paws; pink rayon paw pads; red felt jacket, boots and hat; black felt pants (an integral part of body); glass eyes; f.j.; e.s. Schuco identification tag attached to chest with ribbon. Rare felt "boots" design.
CONDITION: Excellent   PRICE: $3500-up
Yes/No Bear. Circa 1926. 5in (13cm); short pale gold mohair covers metal body; black metal eyes; f.j.; attached metal "spectacles." Head nods "yes" or "no" when tail is moved.
CONDITION: Excellent   PRICE: $1000-up
Yes/No Bear. Circa 1930. 5in (13cm); short beige-colored mohair covers metal frame; glass eyes; f.j. Head nods "yes" or "no" when tail is moved.
CONDITION: Excellent   PRICE: $650-up
Yes/No Bear. Circa 1950. 5in (13cm); short pale gold mohair covers metal body; red felt tongue; glass eyes; f.j. Head nods "yes" or "no" when tail is moved.
CONDITION: Excellent   PRICE: $550-up
Yes/No Bear. Circa 1950. 14in (36cm); beige-colored mohair; glass eyes; f.j.; e.s. Head nods "yes" or "no" when tail is moved. Rare in this condition and with original box.
CONDITION: Mint   PRICE: $2300-up
Courtesy Patricia Volpe.

(Left) Yes/No Bear. Circa 1925. 15in (38cm); pale gold mohair tipped with vivid green; glass eyes; f.j.; e.s. Head nods "yes" or "no" when tail is moved. Rare color.
CONDITION: Excellent   PRICE: $3500-up
(Right) Yes/No Bear. Circa 1925. 17in (43cm); vivid purple tipped with pale gold-colored mohair; glass eyes; f.j.; e.s. Head nods "yes" or "no" when tail is moved. Rare color.
CONDITION: Excellent   PRICE: $4500-up
Courtesy Donna Harrison-West. Photograph by Ho Phi Le.

Yes/No Bear. Circa 1930. 16in (41cm); short bristle-type gold mohair; glass eyes; f.j.; e.s. Head nods "yes" or "no" when tail is moved.
CONDITION: Good
PRICE: $800-up
Private collection.

(Left) Walking Bear. Circa 1930. 10in (25cm); short gold mohair; shoe-button eyes; jointed arms; stationary legs and head; e.s. head and arms; metal body and legs; red felt jacket an integral part of bear's body. Key-wound mechanism concealed in body. When key is wound, bear walks forward on small wheels under soles of black metal shoes. Rare.
CONDITION: Excellent
PRICE: $2500-up
(Right) Dancing Bear. Circa 1930. Short gold mohair head and upper torso and red felt pants cover metal body; black metal eyes. Clockwork mechanism concealed in body. When wound with a key, bear dances in circular motion.
CONDITION: Excellent
PRICE: $1000-up
Courtesy Barbara Baldwin.

Tricky Yes/No Bear. Circa 1950. Beige mohair; glass eyes; f.j.; e.s. Head nods "yes" or "no" when tail is moved. Red plastic tag reads: "Schuco 'Tricky' Patent ANG." Reverse of tag: "D.B. Pat. ang. IND. Patents pending/Made in U.S. Zone Germany."
CONDITION: Excellent
PRICE: 8in (20cm) $650-up
          12in (31cm) $950-up
          17in (43cm) $1600-up
          20in (51cm) $2100-up

(Right) Yes/No Rolley Bear. Circa 1950. 9in (23cm); short beige mohair; glass eyes; f.j. Key wind clockwork movement concealed in tummy; with aid of a stick bear moves backwards and forwards. Marked on base of foot "Made in US - Zone Germany D.R.G.M./Schuco - Rolly."
CONDITION: Excellent   PRICE: $800-up
(Center left) Yes/No Elephant. Circa 1926. 8in (20cm) by 10in (25cm); short gray mohair; glass eyes; unjointed legs; movable head; e.s.; metal wheels ("Schuco-Patent" embossed on wheels). Head nods "yes" or "no" when tail is moved.

CONDITION: Excellent   PRICE: $550-up
(Back right) Tricky Yes/No Dwarf. 11in (28cm); felt face with painted features; white mohair beard; black metal eyes; metal spectacles; made-to-the-body felt and velveteen clothes. Head nods "yes" or "no" when tail is moved.
CONDITION: Excellent   PRICE: $750-up
(Right front) Yes/No Elephant. 5in (13cm); short gray mohair; gray felt ears; glass eyes; f.j.; e.s. Head nods "yes" or "no" when tail is moved.
CONDITION: Excellent   PRICE: $350-up

Yes/No Musical Bear. Circa 1950. 16in (41cm); beige-colored mohair; glass eyes; "rubber" nose; f.j. Music box (concealed in stomach) is activated by turning key located on stomach.
CONDITION: Excellent
PRICE: $1900-up
Private Collection.

Yes/No Bears dressed as Dutch boy and girl. Circa 1950. 8in (20cm); caramel-colored mohair heads, paws and legs; cotton fabric bodies, arms and tops of legs; glass eyes; f.j.; e.s.; original clothes. Heads nod "yes" or "no" when tails are moved.
CONDITION: Excellent
PRICE: $1500-up (each)
Private collection.

Schuco Look-A-Like (German) Bear. Circa 1950. 20in (51cm); pale gold mohair; short pale gold mohair in-set snout and paw pads; glass eyes; f.j.; e.s.
CONDITION: Excellent   **PRICE:** $650-up
Courtesy Marge Adolphson.

Acrobat Bear. Circa 1960. 5½in (14cm); short pale beige mohair covers metal body; black metal eyes; jointed arms and legs; stationary head. Clockwork mechanism concealed in body. When arms are wound in circular motion, bear does somersaults. Original box.
CONDITION: Mint
PRICE: $750-up
Courtesy Barbara Baldwin.

OPPOSITE PAGE:
1992. 14in (36cm); golden-colored silky mohair; plexi-glass eyes; f.j.; s.s.; pull-string voice box. Limited edition of 1000. Manufactured by Bamberger Puppenwerkstätte 1882. Produced under license of Schuco. Comes with certificate hand signed by Eric Kluge.
CONDITION: Mint
PRICE: $225-up
Courtesy E & M Kluge.

ABOVE:
(Left) Rabbit. Circa 1950. 13in (33cm); tan and beige mohair; plastic eyes; red plastic nose; n.j.; flexible arms and legs; s.s.
CONDITION: Excellent   PRICE: $85-up
(Right) Bigo Bello Talking Bear. Circa 1960. 15in (38cm); beige synthetic plush; plastic eyes; black plastic nose; felt lined open mouth; n.j.; s.s. Original label reads: "Schuco bigo bello Parlo." Pull cord activates speaking mechanism (speaking mechanism produced in U.S.A. by Mattel).
CONDITION: Excellent   PRICE: $350-up
Courtesy Karen Strickland.

Yes/No Panda. Circa 1948. 8in (20cm); black and white mohair; glass eyes; f.j.; e.s. Head nods "yes" and "no" when tail is moved.
CONDITION: Excellent PRICE: $1000-up

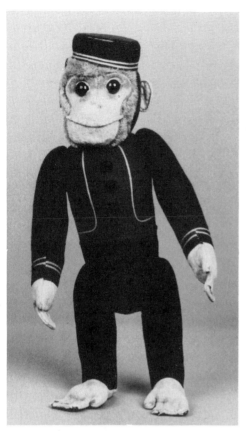

Yes/No Bell Hop Monkey. Circa 1926; short brown mohair; beige felt face and paws; red felt jacket and hat; black felt pants (clothes an integral part of body); glass eyes; f.j.; e.s. Head nods "yes" or "no" when tailed is moved.
CONDITION: Excellent
PRICE: 8in (20cm) $375-up
         12in (31cm) $475-up
         17in (43cm) $550-up
         20in (51cm) $675-up

BOTTOM:
(Left) Monkey (Flask). Circa 1926. 9in (23cm); short brown mohair head with white mohair beard and red and black felt outfit cover metal body; glass eyes; f.j. When head of monkey is removed, it reveals the top of the flask which has a screw-on cap, useable as a shot cup and a cork stopper.
CONDITION: Excellent
PRICE: $500-up
(Center) Acrobat Monkey. Circa 1920. 15in (38cm) (monkey and stand); short brown mohair head and feet and white mohair beard and red and black felt outfit cover metal body; glass eyes; jointed arms and legs; stationary head. The mechanism ("inertia" a fly wheel weight) is concealed in body. It is activated by twisting the body around in circles. The monkey then does somersaults while holding onto the metal posts.
CONDITION: Excellent
PRICE: $500-up
(Right) Yes/No Monkey. Shnico. Circa 1926. 9in (23cm); short brown mohair head with white mohair beard and red and black felt outfit covers metal body; glass eyes; f.j. Head nods "yes" when tail is moved up and down, "no" when tail is moved from side to side. Mouth opens and closes and monkey makes jibbering sounds when pushed towards body.
CONDITION: Excellent
PRICE: $650-up

ABOVE:
Tricky Yes/No Monkeys. Circa 1950. Dark brown mohair; white mohair chin; glass eyes; f.j.; e.s. Heads nod "yes" or "no" when tails are moved. Red plastic tag reads: "Schuco 'Tricky' Patent ANG." Reverse of tag: "D.B. Pat. ang. IND. Patents pending/Made in U.S. Zone Germany."
CONDITION: Excellent
PRICE: 8in (20cm) $125-up
12in (31cm) $195-up
17in (43cm) $275-up
20in (51cm) $375-up

Yes/No Rabbit. Circa 1950. 15in (38cm); white and beige mohair head; beige mohair arms; cotton fabric body; glass eyes; red stitched nose and mouth; f.j.; e.s. Red plastic tag sewn onto clothing reads: "Schuco/Tricky/U.S. Zone/Germany." Dressed in felt vest and slippers with cotton shirt and pants. Head nods "yes" or "no" when tail is moved.
CONDITION: Mint   **PRICE:** $600-up
Courtesy Barbara Baldwin.

(Left to right) Turtle. Circa 1950. 2in (5cm); beige plush covers cardboard form; airbrushed design; pipe cleaner legs; black metal eyes.
CONDITION: Mint **PRICE:** $150-up
Squirrel. Circa 1950; 2½in (3cm); brown and beige mohair covers metal head and body; pipe cleaner legs; black metal eyes.
CONDITION: Mint **PRICE:** $150-up
Circa 1950. 2½in (3cm); brown mohair covers metal head and body; black metal eyes; f.j.; gold metal crown affixed to head; original sash across chest.

CONDITION: Mint **PRICE:** $175-up
Penguin. Circa 1950. 2½in (6cm); white mohair covers metal head and body; airbrushed gray features; black metal eyes.
CONDITION: Mint **PRICE:** $125-up
Poodle. Circa 1950. 2in (5cm); black curly plush covers metal head and body; pipe cleaner legs; glass eyes.
CONDITION: Mint **PRICE:** $165-up
Courtesy Lorraine Fogwell.

(Left) Hare. Circa 1950. 3in (8cm); short pale gold mohair covers metal body; pink felt lined ears; black metal eyes; red stitched nose and mouth; f.j.
CONDITION: Excellent **PRICE:** $150-up
(Center) Yes/No Cat. Circa 1935. 9in (22cm); white mohair tipped with gray; black and white googly eyes; f.j. Head nods "yes" or "no" when tail is moved. Original paper tag attached to cat pictures Schuco's logo and an illustration of the yes/no action.
CONDITION: Excellent **PRICE:** $875-up
Tiger. Circa 1950. 3in (8cm) long; short beige mohair (airbrushed stripes) covers metal body; green glass eyes; f.j.
CONDITION: Excellent **PRICE:** $150-up

(Left) Yes/No Cat. Circa 1930. 8in (20cm); white mohair (originally was tipped in a color); yellow glass eyes; pink stitched nose and mouth; unjointed legs; e.s. Head nods "yes" or "no" when tail is moved.
CONDITION: Excellent **PRICE:** $1000-up
(Right) Yes/No Fox Terrier Dog. Circa 1930. 10in (25cm); black and white mohair; black and white glass eyes; unjointed legs; e.s. Head nods "yes" or "no" when tail is moved.
CONDITION: Excellent **PRICE:** $750-up
Private collection.

Yes/No Cats. Circa 1950. 8in (20cm); short gray mohair; black mohair ears; pink cotton stitched nose; green glass eyes; f.j.; e.s. Red plastic tags sewn onto chest reads: "Schuco/Tricky/U.S. Zone/ Germany." Heads nod "yes" or"no" when tail is moved. (Cat on right) Dressed in black felt pants and cotton red and white striped sweater.
CONDITION: Excellent
PRICE: $425-up (each)
Courtesy Barbara Baldwin.

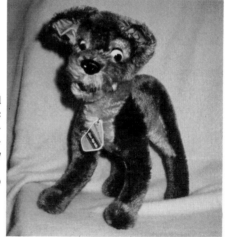

Dog. Circa 1958. 13in (33cm); short brown and white mohair; plastic eyes glancing to side; plastic nose; n.j.; e.s. Tag affixed to chest reads: "Original Walt Disney. Schuco bigo-bello" Dog represents Tramp from the Walt Disney® movie *Lady and the Tramp.*
CONDITION: Mint   PRICE: $300-up
Courtesy Darleen Foote.

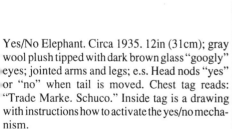

Yes/No Elephant. Circa 1935. 12in (31cm); gray wool plush tipped with dark brown glass "googly" eyes; jointed arms and legs; e.s. Head nods "yes" or "no" when tail is moved. Chest tag reads: "Trade Marke. Schuco." Inside tag is a drawing with instructions how to activate the yes/no mechanism.
CONDITION: Excellent   PRICE: $750-up
Private collection.

Steiff

The oldest and most famous of all bear manufacturers is the Steiff Company which is most often credited with introducing the first movable toy bear at the Leipzig Toy Fair in 1903.

Steiff bears of the early period are without a doubt one of the most valuable and collectible bears today. Easily identifiable with an elongated nose, arms, feet and hump, they are highly coveted and difficult to locate.

The post-war trade boom, was Steiff's heydey for exportation. The U.S. market was ripe for its products during the 1950s. It is animals from this decade that a large percentage of collectors seek today.

Steiff Bears

Steiff "Rod" Bear (35PB). Circa 1904. 19¾in (50cm); long silky apricot-colored mohair; large shoe-button eyes; diagonal seam at top of head; f.j.; metal rods connect joints; e.s.; body extremely hard; elephant button. Originally had sealing wax nose. Extremely rare.
CONDITION: Excellent
PRICE: Sold at Sotheby's May 1991 auction
         for £11,770 (approximately $23,000)

Steiff Rod Bear 28 PB. Circa 1904. 16in (41cm); long silky honey-colored mohair; large button eyes; diagonal seam at top of head; f.j.; metal rods connect joints; e.s.; body extremely hard; sealing wax nose; five embroidered claw stitches; septum and mouth are of thin light tan thread; elephant button. X-ray in illustration taken from this bear.
CONDITION: Excellent
PRICE: $15,000-up

Price guide for Steiff's basic teddy bear design produced from 1905 to 1910 in honey-colored mohair with shoe-button eyes.

	Mint Condition	Good Condition	Fair Condition
10in (25cm)	$1800-up	$1000-up	$500-up
16in (41cm)	$3500-up	$2000-up	$1200-up
20in (51cm)	$5000-up	$3500-up	$2000-up
24in (61cm)	$7000-up	$5000-up	$3000-up
28in (71cm)	$11,000-up	$7000-up	$4500-up

Note: Facial appeal and rare colors could command higher prices.

(Bears left to right) Steiff. Circa 1905. 16in (40cm); white mohair; shoe-button eyes; tan-colored pearl cotton stitched nose, mouth and claws; f.j.; kapok and excelsior stuffing; FF button. Early teddy bears produced in white mohair are among the most collectible of Steiff bears today.
CONDITION: Excellent   PRICE: $3800-up
(Center) Steiff Bear. Circa 1910. 8in (20cm); white mohair; small shoe-button eyes; tan-colored stitched nose, mouth and claws; f.j.; e.s.; FF button.
CONDITION: Mint   PRICE: $1500-up
(Right) Steiff Bear. Circa 1905. 14in (35cm); white mohair; shoe-button eyes; tan-colored pearl cotton stitched nose, mouth and claws; f.j.; kapok and excelsior stuffing; blank button; white S.L.
CONDITION: Mint   PRICE: $3500-up
Jumeau Doll. Circa 1880. 20in (51cm); bisque head; incised on back of head "Depose E.9.J.;" blue glass paper-weight eyes; closed mouth; composition body; straight wrists; clothes not original.
CONDITION: Excellent   PRICE: $8000-up
Pruitts Place. "Goose Caboose." 1983. 14in (36cm); tall by 32in (81cm) long; carved wood; natural hand rubbed finish; plastic eyes. Limited edition 1500.
CONDITION: Mint   PRICE: $375-up

(Left) Steiff Bear on Metal Wheels. Circa 1905. 6½in (15cm) tall by 9in (23cm) long; brown burlap; shoe-button eyes; unjointed legs; swivel head; e.s.
CONDITION: Good   **PRICE:** $800-up

(Right) Steiff Bear on Wooden Wheels. Circa 1913. 9in (23cm) tall by 11½in (29cm) long; brown burlap; shoe-button eyes; unjointed legs; stationary head; e.s.; FF button.
CONDITION: Excellent   **PRICE:** $1300-up
Private collection.

Steiff Bear Puppet. Circa 1912. 9in (23cm); short gold mohair; shoe-button eyes; n.j.; e.s. head; FF button.
CONDITION: Excellent   **PRICE:** $1000-up
Private collection.

Steiff (Tumbling) Bear. Circa 1913. 13in (33cm); honey-colored mohair; shoe-button eyes; f.j.; e.s.; FF button; mechanical mechanism concealed in body. Arms wind clockwork mechanism to activate tumbling motion.
CONDITION: Good   **PRICE:** $3000-up
Courtesy Ho Phi Le.

Steiff Bear. Circa 1908. 28in (71cm); honey-
colored mohair; large button eyes; f.j.; <u>FF</u> button.
CONDITION: Mint   **PRICE:** $11,000-up
Courtesy Barbara Lauver.

Steiff Bear. Circa 1910. 18in (46cm); gray mohair (probably originally brown); shoe-button eyes; f.j.; e.s. Rare color.
CONDITION: Excellent   **PRICE:** $3500-up
Steiff. Wooly Mammoth. Circa 1920. Approximate size 9in (23cm); short bright red mohair; glass eyes; n.j.; e.s.; FF button.
CONDITION: Excellent   **PRICE:** $800-up
Private collection.

Steiff Bear. Circa 1910. 20in (64cm); white mohair; shoe-button eyes; f.j.; e.s.; FF button. Note the loss of hair on right arm. Probably worn from constantly being held in the same place.
CONDITION: Fair   **PRICE:** $2000-up

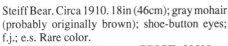

(Left to right) Steiff Clown Doll. Circa 1910. 17in (46cm); beige felt face and hands; shoe-button eyes; f.j.; e.s. gold mohair; orange and yellow felt clown outfit.
CONDITION: Good
PRICE: $1500-up
(Center) Steiff Bear. Circa 1907. 28in (71cm); long wavy soft light brown colored mohair; shoe-button eyes; f.j.; e.s.; FF button.
CONDITION: Excellent
PRICE: $9000-up
(Right) German Clown Doll. Circa 1910. 13in (33cm); beige felt face and hands; black and purple silk outfit (an integral part of the body); shoe-button eyes; jointed arms and stationary legs; swivel head; e.s.
CONDITION: Good
PRICE: $500-up

(Left) Steiff Bear. Circa 1925. 24in (61cm); long silky brown mohair; glass eyes; f.j.; e.s.; FF button.
CONDITION: Excellent   PRICE: $6000-up
(Center left) Steiff Bear. Circa 1905. 16in (41cm); long silky apricot mohair; f.j.; five stitched claws; excelsior and kapok stuffing; blank button. Desirable color and early design.
CONDITION: Mint   PRICE: $5000-up

(Center and center right) Steiff Bears. Circa 1908. 30in (76cm); long silky rich golden-colored mohair; large button eyes; f.j.; e.s.; FF button.
CONDITION: Mint   PRICE: $12,000-up (each)
(Right) Steiff Bear. Circa 1905. 20in (51cm); long silky apricot-colored mohair; glass eyes; center seam in head; f.j.; e.s.; FF button.
CONDITION: Excellent   PRICE: $6000-up
Private collection. Photograph courtesy Teddy Bear and friends®

(Left) Steiff Bear. Circa 1912. 12in (31cm); gold mohair; shoe-button eyes; f.j.; e.s.; automatic (tilt-type) voice box (unusual for 12in [31cm] bears from this era). The majority have squeeze type cry box (squeaker). FF button.
CONDITION: Excellent   PRICE: $1500-up
(Right) Steiff Bear. Circa 1912. 12in (31cm); black mohair; shoe-button eyes; black pearl cotton nose and mouth; f.j.; e.s. FF button. This bear and the bear on the left are the same design as the Richard Steiff bear (known as Gray Richard). A percentage of black Steiff bears were produced with red felt circles under the black button eyes. Rare.
CONDITION: Excellent   PRICE: $10,000-up
Private collection.

ABOVE:
Steiff Goat. Circa 1913. 16in (41cm); blonde mohair; green glass eyes; f.j.; e.s.
CONDITION: Fair
PRICE: $500-up
Steiff Bear. Circa 1910. 10in (25cm); honey-colored mohair; shoe-button eyes; f.j.; e.s.
CONDITION: Good
PRICE: $800-up
Steiff Gnome. "Snik." Circa 1913. 8in (20cm); beige felt face (painted features) and body; glass eyes; f.j.; e.s.; felt clothes.
CONDITION: Excellent
PRICE: $950-up
Courtesy Mimi Hiscox.

Steiff Bear. Circa 1912. 20in (51cm); black silky mohair; shoe-button eyes backed with red felt; center seam in head; f.j.; e.s.; <u>FF</u> button. Extremely rare. It appears approximately 12 black bears were produced with the desirable center seam.
CONDITION: Excellent
PRICE: Sold at Sotheby's May 1990 Auction for approximately $41,000.
Private collection.

(Left) Steiff Bear. Circa 1907. 29in (74cm); long silky white mohair; large button eyes; f.j.; e.s.; FF button. Rare size.
CONDITION: Excellent   **PRICE:** $11,000-up
Steiff Golliwog. Circa 1913. 19in (48cm); black felt face with formed nose; shoe-button eyes; surrounded by white and red felt circles; red felt applied mouth; fuzzy black hair; black felt hands; f.j.; e.s.; bright non-removable blue felt jacket, white shirt and vest; loose fitting red trousers. Steiff produced the Golliwog from 1908 until 1917. He was available in seven sizes (11in [28cm] to 39in [99cm]). Very rare.
CONDITION: Excellent   **PRICE:** $11,000-up

Steiff Bear. 1907. 20in (51cm); long curly cinnamon-colored mohair; shoe-button eyes; f.j.; e.s.
CONDITION: Mint   **PRICE:** $6500-up
Courtesy Author (Bear). Bob Collins (July 4th collectibles). Photograph by Bob Collins.

(Front) Steiff Bear. Circa 1905. 12in (31cm); creamy white mohair; shoebutton eyes; f.j.; excelsior and kapok stuffing; FF button.
CONDITION: Excellent
PRICE: $1500-up
(Back) Steiff Bear. Circa 1920. 20in (51cm); white mohair; glass eyes; f.j.; e.s.
CONDITION: Good
PRICE: $3000-up
Courtesy Ho Phi Le.

Steiff Record Teddy Bears. Circa 1913. (Back left) 9in (22cm) long by 10in (25cm) tall; light brown mohair; shoe-button eyes. (Back right) Circa 1929. 10in (25cm) long by 10in (25cm) tall; orange mohair (rare color); glass eyes. (Front left) circa 1913. 4¾in (12cm) long by 5¾in (15cm) tall; pale gold mohair; glass eyes. (Front right) 1930. 6in (15cm) long by 7½in(19cm) tall; gold mohair; glass eyes. All bears are f.j.; e.s.; <u>FF</u> button; metal frames and wooden wheels. Originally introduced in 1912 with a monkey (Record Peter), the popular "Record" series was produced in a variety of animals and character dolls. It proved such a popular design. Steiff continued production well into the 1950s. The figure is seated on a sturdy metal chassis with four wooden wheels and a pair of bellows fitted to the rear axle for the automatic sound effect. When pulled, the figure moves backwards and forwards, creating the appearance the animal is steering himself.
CONDITION: Excellent
PRICE: (Back left) $5000-up
(Back right) $6500-up
(Front left) $3500-up
(Front right) $4000-up
Private collection.

Steiff "Muzzle" Bear. Circa 1913. 13in (33cm); brown mohair; shoe-button eyes; f.j.; e.s.; original leather muzzle. Rare.
CONDITION: Excellent   **PRICE:** $3800-up
Courtesy Barbara Baldwin.

Steiff Polar Bears. Circa 1913. (Left) 13in (33cm) long; (Right) 18in (46cm) long; short white mohair; shoe-button eyes; jointed arms and legs; unjointed "flexible" head; e.s.
CONDITION: Excellent
PRICE: (Left) $2000-up
(Right) $3000-up
Private collection.

Steiff "Dancing Bears." Circa 1920. (Left) 12in (31cm); gold mohair; glass eyes; f.j.; e.s.; FF button. Green felt jacket; orange felt pants. (Right) 10in (25cm); white mohair; glass eyes; f.j.; e.s.; FF button; striped cotton skirt. Rare.
CONDITION: Excellent
PRICE: Sold at Christie's February 1992 auction for £3520 (approximately $7000)
Courtesy Christie's South Kensington, England.

Price guide for Steiff's basic teddy bear design produced from 1915 to 1930 in honey-colored mohair with glass eyes.

	Mint Condition	Good Condition	Fair Condition
10in (25cm)	$1200-up	$800-up	$500-up
16in (41cm)	$2500-up	$2000-up	$1000-up
20in (51cm)	$4000-up	$3000-up	$2000-up
24in (61cm)	$5000-up	$3800-up	$2500-up
28in (71cm)	$8000-up	$6000-up	$4000-up

Note: facial appeal and rare colors could command higher prices.

ABOVE:
(Left) Steiff Bear. Circa 1920. 16in (41cm); white silky mohair; glass eyes; f.j.; e.s.; FF button; white S.L. Rare color.
CONDITION: Mint
PRICE: $3200-up
(Center) Steiff Bear. Circa 1920. 16in (41cm); gold silky mohair; glass eyes; f.j.; e.s.; FF button.
CONDITION: Mint
PRICE: $2500-up
(Right) Steiff Bear. Circa 1920. 16in (41cm); long silky gray mohair (originally brown); glass eyes; f.j.; e.s.; FF button. Rare color.
CONDITION: Excellent
PRICE: $3200-up
Pruitt Place Leaf. 1990. Carved wood (painted green). 21in (53cm) by 9in (23cm).
CONDITION: Mint
PRICE: $125-up

Steiff Bear. Circa 1920. 28in (71cm); gold (faded) mohair; glass eyes; f.j.; e.s.; FF button. Extremely appealing round face.
CONDITION: Excellent
PRICE: $7000-up
Private collection.

(Left) Steiff Bear. Circa 1930. 35in (89cm); white "cotton" plush; glass eyes; brown pearl cotton stitched nose, mouth and claws; f.j.; s.s. Rare size, especially in cotton plush.
CONDITION: Good
PRICE: $4500-up
(Right) Käthe Kruse Doll. 1950. 45in (114cm).
CONDITION: Excellent
PRICE: $2000-up
Courtesy Brigitte Nohrudi.

Steiff Bear. Circa 1930. 13in (33cm); gold mohair glass eyes; f.j.; e.s.; <u>FF</u> button; red S.L.
CONDITION: Mint
PRICE: $2400-up
Courtesy Barbara Baldwin.

Steiff "Teddy Baby" Bear. Circa 1931. 7in (18cm); white mohair; short mohair inset snout; beige felt lined open mouth; pale beige velveteen feet; "orange" glass eyes; rust-colored pearl cotton stitched nose; f.j.; e.s.; original collar, bell and Steiff identification C.T. White Teddy Babies were produced from 1930 to 1932. Rare color.
CONDITION: Excellent   **PRICE:** $2000-up
Private collection.

Steiff "Teddy Clown" Bear. Circa 1926. 10in (25cm); pale beige mohair; shoe-button eyes; f.j.; e.s.; FF button; original beige felt clown hat; two colored ruff. Rare. Steiff produced the Teddy Clown in eleven sizes from 9in (23cm) to 45in (114cm) in colors beige tipped in brown, pink and gold mohair.
CONDITION: Excellent   **PRICE:** $4000-up
Steiff Pig. Circa 1928. 6in (15cm) tall; white mohair; glass eyes; n.j.; e.s.; original two-colored ruff; FF button; red S.L. Rare.
CONDITION: Mint   **PRICE:** $1000-up
Private collection.

Steiff "Teddy Clown" Bear. Circa 1926. 11in (36cm); pale beige mohair; glass eyes; f.j.; e.s.; FF button; white C.T. reads: "teddyclown." Felt clown hat with red silk pom poms. Two-colored silk ruff. Very rare, especially with "white" C.T.
CONDITION: Mint   **PRICE:** $6000-up
Courtesy Barbara Baldwin.

(Left) Steiff Petsy Bear. Circa 1927. 18in (46cm); white mohair tipped with reddish-brown; blue glass eyes; red stitched pearl cotton nose and mouth; f.j.; s.s. with wool shearings; <u>FF</u> button; remnants of white S.L. Rare.
CONDITION: Excellent
PRICE: $10,000-up
(Center) Steiff Record Petsy Bear. Circa 1928. 10in (25cm) tall; white mohair tipped with reddish-brown; blue glass eyes; red stitched pearl cotton nose and mouth; f.j.; e.s.; <u>FF</u> button; remnants of white S.L. Rare.
CONDITION: Excellent
PRICE: $12,000-up
(Right) Steiff Petsy Bear. Circa 1928. 18in (46cm); white mohair tipped with reddish-brown; blue and white glass googly eyes; red stitched pearl cotton nose,mouth and claws;

f.j.; s.s. with wool shearings; <u>FF</u> button. Characteristics of Petsy's are oversized posable ears fitted with wires; seams run down from the center, front, back and crosswise from ear to back; v-shaped gusset from center of mouth to neck.
CONDITION: Excellent   **PRICE:** $10,000-up
Private collection.

Steiff "Tretomobil" Childs' Pedal Car. Circa 1929. 42in (107cm) long; sheet metal body finished in gray with opening door, maroon running boards (repainted) cast steering wheel, small electric headlamps and spotlamp, rear view mirror, manual turn signals, horn (replaced) number plate 111Y 1929, maroon leather covered seat, black rubber tires on flat wheel rims, windscreen (replaced) with wiper blade, complete with spare rubber tire and tool kit in leather case. Extremely rare.

CONDITION: Excellent
PRICE: Sold at Sotheby's May 1991 auction for £5060 (approximately $10,000).
Steiff Bear. Circa 1925; 29 in (74cm); honey-colored mohair (replaced mohair paws and felt pads); glass eyes; f.j.; e.s.
CONDITION: Good
PRICE: Included in Sotheby's May 1991 auction with an estimated price of $1500. Bear was withdrawn from auction.
Courtesy Sotheby's.

This group of miniature Steiff bears depict the changes in Steiff's miniature bear designs from 1905 to 1960. All examples are approximately 3½in (9cm) tall; shades of honey-colored mohair (with the exception of the center bear which is the rare white mohair); tiny black button eyes; f.j.; e.s. Note how the length of the mohair and the shape of the faces change over the years.

CONDITION: Excellent
PRICE: (Left) Circa 1910 $600-up
(Second left) Circa 1925 $500-up
(Center) Circa 1940 $600-up
(Second right) Circa 1952 $350-up
(Right) Circa 1960 $250-up
Private collection.

(Right) Steiff "Dicky" Bear. Circa 1930. 16in (41cm); blonde-colored mohair with short mohair plush in-set snout; painted paw pads (design somewhat worn); f.j.; e.s.; FF button; remnants of red S.L.

CONDITION: Excellent
PRICE: $10,000-up
(Center) Steiff "Dicky" Bear. Circa 1930. 12in (31cm); white mohair with short mohair plush in-set snout; velveteen paw pads with painted paw designs; glass eyes; f.j.; e.s.; FF button; remnants of red label.
CONDITION: Excellent
PRICE: $8000-up
(Left) Steiff "Dicky" Bear. Circa 1930. 9in (23cm); gold mohair with corn-gold short mohair plush in-set snout; felt pads; glass eyes; f.j.; e.s.; FF button; remnants of red S.L. Rare.
CONDITION: Excellent
PRICE: $6000-up
Private collection.

Steiff Bear (Movable Head Mechanism). Circa 1933. 9in (23cm) tall; rich dark brown mohair; short beige mohair in-set snout; glass eyes; unjointed body; e.s.; FF button; with remnants of red S.L. Originally a tag was attached to the tail which read: "Turn here and I will move my head." Rare.
CONDITION: Excellent
PRICE: $3500-up
Private collection.

Steiff "Circus Bear." (Movable Head Mechanism). Circa 1935. 13in (33cm); long rich brown mohair; short beige in-set snout; glass eyes; jointed arms and legs (paws turn down); mechanical head (head moves in circular motion when tail is turned); e.s. Rare. Steiff produced 897 examples of the Circus Bear in one size only from 1935 until 1939.
CONDITION: Mint
PRICE: $5000-up
Private collection.

Steiff Bear. Circa 1936. 18in (46cm); white mohair; glass eyes; brown pearl cotton stitched nose, mouth and claws; f.j.; e.s.; FF button; yellow S.L. Rare color and condition.
CONDITION: Mint
PRICE: $3800-up
Courtesy Barbara Baldwin.

ABOVE:
(Left) Steiff Teddy Doll. Circa 1945. 8in (20cm); beige wool plush head, hands and feet; linen body; felt lined open mouth; glass eyes; stationary arms and legs; swivel head; e.s.; red felt jacket; white linen shirt; dark blue felt trousers.
CONDITION: Excellent
PRICE: $1500-up
(Right) Steiff "Nimrod" Bear. Circa 1954. 8in (20cm); honey-colored mohair; glass eyes; f.j.; e.s.; R.S.B.; yellow S.L.; C.T. Original hunting outfit; green felt shirt; orange felt hat; brown leather boots and gun.
CONDITION: Mint
PRICE: $1500-up
Courtesy Patricia Volpe.

Steiff Bear. Circa 1945. 13in (33cm); pale gold "cotton" plush; glass eyes; f.j.; printed (block) STEIFF button without F underscored.
CONDITION: Excellent
PRICE: $850-up
Courtesy Barbara Baldwin.

(Left) Steiff Teddy Baby Bear. Circa 1945. 11in (28cm); gold "cotton" plush; glass eyes; brown stitched nose and claws; rayon paw pads; f.j.; e.s.; printed (block) STEIFF button (no F underscored).
CONDITION: Good
PRICE: $1400-up
(Center front) Steiff Teddy Baby Bear. Circa 1947. 11in (28cm); light gold mohair; glass eyes; f.j.; e.s.; R.S.B.; yellow S.L. "U.S. Zone Germany" label sewn into seam of body.
CONDITION: Excellent
PRICE: $1200-up
(Right) Steiff Teddy Baby Bear. Circa 1960. 16in (41cm); cream-colored mohair; glass eyes; dark brown stitched nose, mouth and claws; beige ultra suede pads; f.j.; s.s.; R.S.B.; yellow S.L.
CONDITION: Excellent
PRICE: $1900-up
Courtesy Barbara Baldwin.

These examples of Steiff teddy bears represent the slight changes of Steiff's basic design from 1945 to 1960. (Left) Steiff Bear. Circa 1945. 11in (28cm); gold mohair; glass eyes; f.j.; e.s. Label under arm reads: "U.S. Zone Germany."
CONDITION: Excellent   PRICE: $350-up
(Center front) Steiff Bear. Circa 1950. 13in (33cm); white mohair; glass eyes; f.j.; e.s.
CONDITION: Excellent   PRICE: $400-up

(Right) Steiff Bear. Circa 1950. 13in (33cm); caramel-colored mohair; glass eyes; f.j.; e.s.
CONDITION: Excellent   PRICE: $300-up
(Back center) Steiff Bear. Circa 1960. 14in (36cm); gold mohair; glass eyes; f.j.; e.s.
CONDITION: Excellent   PRICE: $300-up

Steiff Original Teddy. Circa 1950. Caramel-colored mohair; glass eyes; f.j.; e.s.; R.S.B.; C.T.
CONDITION: Mint
PRICE: 10in (25cm) $350-up
16in (41cm) $600-up
26in (66cm) $2500-up
30in (76cm) $3000-up
Rare colors command higher prices.

Steiff "Teddy Baby" (Musical) Bear. Circa 1951. 9in (23cm); head and arms dark brown mohair; short beige mohair in-set snout; beige felt lined open mouth; short blonde mohair body; glass eyes; unjointed arms; swivel head; e.s.; tube body conceals music box; bellows produces music when tube body is pressed in downward motion. Dress not original. Originally dressed in Bavarian-style blouse and skirt. Rare.
CONDITION: Excellent   **PRICE:** $2000-up
Private collection.

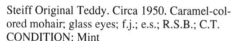

Steiff "Jackie Bears." Circa 1953. (Left) 7in (18cm); (Center) 10in (25cm); (Right) 14in (36cm); blonde-colored mohair; glass eyes; f.j.; e.s.; R.S.B. Created as Steiff's first jubilee bear. Identifying features are dark shaded area for navel, pink silk stitch horizontally sewn across nose.
CONDITION: Excellent
PRICE: 7in (18cm) $950-up
10in (25cm) $1250-up
14in (36cm) $1500-up
Private collection.

OPPOSITE PAGE:
A representation of the various colors Steiff produced the popular Zotty bear during the 1950s. The following information is for the most-common caramel-colored version.
Steiff Zotty Bear. Circa 1950. Long silky caramel-colored mohair tipped with white; short caramel mohair in-set snout; gold mohair chest; pink felt lined open mouth; glass eyes; f.j.; paws turned in downward position; e.s.; R.S.B.

	Mint Condition	Good Condition	Worn Condition
9in (23cm)	$275-up	$175-up	$100-up
14in (36cm)	$450-up	$300-up	$150-up
20in (51cm)	$650-up	$400-up	$200-up

Note: Rare colors command higher prices.

(Back row left) Steiff Panda. Circa 1950. 12in (31cm); black and white mohair; open pink felt lined mouth; glass eyes; f.j.; paws turned in downward position; gray suede paw pads; e.s.; R.S.B.; yellow S.L.; original ribbon.
CONDITION: Mint
PRICE: $1600-up
(Back row right) Steiff Panda. Circa 1950. 14in (36cm); black and white mohair; open pink felt lined mouth; glass eyes; f.j.; paws turned in downward position; gray suede paw pads; e.s.; R.S.B.
CONDITION: Excellent
PRICE: $1200-up

(Front row left) Steiff Panda. Circa 1950. 8in (20cm); black and white mohair; pink felt lined open mouth; glass eyes; f.j.; paws turned in downward position; gray suede pads; e.s.; R.S.B.; yellow S.L.; C.T.
CONDITION: Mint
PRICE: $1300-up
(Front row right) Steiff Panda. Circa 1950. 6in (15cm); black and white mohair; pink felt lined open mouth; glass eyes; f.j.; paws turned in downward position; beige felt paw pads; e.s.; R.S.B.; C.T.
CONDITION: Mint
PRICE: $850-up
Courtesy Barbara Baldwin.

Steiff Bear on Wheels. Circa 1960. 30in (76cm) long by 24in (61cm) high; brown mohair; short beige mohair face; glass eyes; brown stitched nose and mouth; n.j.; e.s.; metal frame; red painted metal disc wheels; white rubber tires.
CONDITION: Excellent
PRICE: $650-up
Courtesy Brigitte Nohrudi.

Steiff Original Teddy Bear. Circa 1970. Caramel-colored mohair; short mohair heart-shaped face; glass eyes; f.j.; synthetic pads; e.s.; I.B.
CONDITION: Excellent
PRICE: 10in (25cm) $75-up
16in (41cm) $125-up
26in (66cm) $250-up
30in (76cm) $475-up
Rare Colors and C.T. command higher prices.

Since the Margarete Steiff Company's 100th anniversary in 1980, the company has launched a program of Limited Edition replicas of old Steiff items.The major portion of this series is comprised of teddy bears. The first limited edition was the Jubilee (Papa) Bear. The great success of this very first teddy bear replica from Steiff gave rise to the "Mama and Baby" set the following year.

(Right) Steiff Jubilee (Papa) Bear. 1980. 17in (43cm); gold-colored mohair; black plastic eyes; f.j.; e.s.; *Steiff* incised in script on large brass button; white woven S.L.; boxed with certificate. Limited edition of 11,000 pieces world wide. Of this edition 5000 have an English certificate and were only sold in America.
CONDITION: Mint   PRICE: $825-up
(Left) Steiff "Mama and Baby" set. 1981. Mama. 15in (38cm). Baby. 6in (15cm); gold-colored mohair; black plastic eyes; f.j.; s.s.; Steiff incised on large brass button; white woven S.L.; originally an orange ribbon encircled mother and baby with the words "Margarete Steiff/KNOPF IM OHR/Ltd Edition;" boxed with certificate. Limited edition of 8000 pieces with an English certificate available only in America.
CONDITION: Mint   PRICE: $550-up

(Left front) Steiff "Snap-A-Part" Bear. 1989-1991. Replica 1909. 6¾in (17cm); white mohair; black plastic eyes; f.j.; e.s.; limbs can be pulled away from body and interchanged with any other part; *Steiff* incised in script on large brass button; white printed ribbon S.L.; boxed with certificate. Limited edition of 5000 pieces.
CONDITION: Mint   PRICE: $185-up
(Right front) Steiff Jackie Bear. 1989. Replica 1953. 6¾in (17cm); beige mohair; shaded brown navel; brown stitched nose (vertical pink stitch across nose), mouth and claws; f.j.; e.s.; *Steiff* incised in script on large brass button; white printed ribbon S.L. Limited edition 12,000.
CONDITION: Mint   PRICE: $145-up
(Left back) Steiff "Richard" Bear. 1982. Replica 1905. 12in (32cm); gray mohair; black plastic

eyes; f.j.; s.s.; *Steiff* incised in script on large brass button; white woven S.L.; boxed with certificate. Limited edition 20,000.
CONDITION: Mint   PRICE: $325-up
(Right back) Steiff Clifford Berryman Bear. 1987. 13in (35cm); brown mohair; white mohair in-set snout; felt lined open mouth; black and white plastic "googly" eyes; f.j.; s.s.; airbrushed paw pads; *Steiff* incised in script on large brass button; yellow cloth-weave S.L. Discontinued. To commemorate renowned cartoonist Clifford Berryman's immortal portrayal of Teddy Roosevelt's 1902 bear hunt in Mississippi, Linda Mullins, together with the Steiff company, created the 85th Anniversary Clifford Berryman bear.
CONDITION: Mint   PRICE: $250-up

(Left) Steiff Bear. 1988. 84in (213cm); honey-colored mohair; large glass eyes; f.j. (jointed with metal rods); s.s.; *Steiff* incised in script on large brass button; white printed ribbon S.L.; 197 Steiff buttons affixed to collar. One-of-a-kind. Created for the first Walt Disney World® Teddy Bear Convention.
CONDITION: Mint
PRICE: $2600-up
(Right) Steiff Bear. 1989. 60in (152cm); white mohair; large glass eyes; f.j. (jointed with metal rods); s.s.; *Steiff* incised in script on large brass button; white printed ribbon S.L.; 135 small and 11 large Steiff buttons affixed to collar. One-of-a-kind. Created for the second Walt Disney World® Teddy Bear Convention.
CONDITION: Mint
PRICE: $1800-up
(Left front) Steiff. Bicolor Bear. 1990. Replica 1926. 26in (65cm); gray mohair tipped with brown; large plastic eyes; f.j.; e.s.; *Steiff* incised on large brass button; white printed ribbon S.L. Limited edition 5000.
CONDITION: Mint
PRICE: $600-up
Courtesy William and Cynthia Brintnall.

Steiff Bicolor Bear. Replica 1926. (Left) 1990. 26in (65cm); limited edition 5000. (Right) 1991. 15¾in (40cm); limited edition 6000. Gray mohair tipped with brown; large plastic eyes; f.j.; e.s. Steiff incised on large brass button; white printed ribbon S.L.
CONDITION: Mint
PRICE: (Left) 26in (65cm) $600-up
        (Right) 15¾in (40cm) $395-up
Courtesy Steiff.

Steiff "Baerle." Bear 35 PB. 1991. Replica 1903. 19¾in (50cm); distressed cinnamon-colored mohair; shoe-button eyes; simulated sealing wax nose; f.j. (twine thread, jointing cardboard discs); e.s. *Steiff* incised in script on large brass button; white printed ribbon S.L. Limited edition 6000 pieces. This replica was the predecessor of the "Metal Rod Bears" of 1904/1905.
CONDITION: Mint   PRICE: $795-up
Courtesy Steiff.

Steiff. Walt Disney World® Convention Bears. (Left to right) Margaret Strong. 1988. 12½in (32cm); honey-colored mohair; plastic eyes; f.j.; s.s.; *Steiff* incised on large brass button; white printed ribbon S.L.; limited edition 1000.
CONDITION: Mint   PRICE: $350-up
Petsy Bear. 1989. 13½in (35cm); white mohair; plastic eyes; f.j.; s.s.; *Steiff* incised in script on large brass button; white printed ribbon S.L.; limited edition 1000.
CONDITION: Mint   PRICE: $300-up

Bear. 1990. 12½in (32cm); charcoal gray mohair; plastic eyes; f.j.; s.s.; *Steiff* incised in script in large brass button; white printed ribbon S.L.; limited edition 1000.
CONDITION: Mint   PRICE: $275-up
Margaret Strong Bear. 1991. 12½in (32cm); black mohair; plastic eyes; f.j.; s.s.; *Steiff* incised in script on large brass button; white printed ribbon S.L. Comes with Mickey Mouse mask. Limited edition 1500.
CONDITION: Mint   PRICE: $275-up
Courtesy William and Cynthia Brintnall.

Steiff Teddy Rose. 1987. 16in (41cm); pink mohair; plastic eyes; center seam in head; brown stitched nose, mouth and claws; f.j.; e.s.; *Steiff* incised in script on large brass button; white cloth-weave S.L. Limited edition 10,000. Replica 1925 design.
CONDITION: Mint   **PRICE:** $325-up
Courtesy Ho Phi Le.

Steiff Animals

Rabbits. (Back left) *Skittle.* Circa 1900. 9in (23cm); beige velveteen; shoe-button eyes; n.j.; e.s.; mounted on a wooden base. Part of a set.
CONDITION: Good
PRICE: $600-up
(Front left) Clothes Brush. Circa 1914. 7¾in (20cm) long by 3½in (9cm) tall; cream-colored velveteen; airbrushed design in brown; red pearl cotton nose and mouth; glass eyes (color painted on back); n.j.; k.s. (firm). Stiff bristle brush. Rare.
CONDITION: Excellent
PRICE: $800-up
(Right) Rabbit. Circa 1913. 11in (28cm); sparse white rough plush; shoe-button eyes; pink pearl cotton nose and mouth; n.j.; e.s.; FF button. Note ear stitching used during this period.
CONDITION: Good
PRICE: $850-up
Private collection.

(Left) **Jack** Rabbit. Circa 1926. 13½in (34cm); cream-colored mohair tipped with brown head and paws; cream mohair in center of forehead; ears are lined with pink velveteen; pink pearl cotton stitched nose and mouth outlined with black thread; black pearl cotton stitched mouth with red felt tongue; glass eyes; jointed arms; stationary legs; swivel head; e.s.; FF button. Produced between 1927 and 1931 in sizes 9in (23cm) to 11in (28cm). Velveteen clothes are not removable. Shoes are brown leather. Rare.
CONDITION: Excellent
PRICE: $3800-up
(Right) Rabbit. Circa 1908. 10in (25cm); cream-colored velveteen; airbrush design in brown; pink pearl cotton stitched nose and mouth; shoe-button eyes backed with red felt; n.j.; k.s.; FF button. Dressed in blue felt coat trimmed with gold braid. Shoes are red felt with leather soles.
CONDITION: Excellent
PRICE: $2000-up
Private collection.

(Left) Rabbit. 1913. 9in (23cm) long by 5in (13cm) tall; tan and white felt; shoe-button eyes backed with red felt; pink pearl cotton stitched nose and mouth; n.j.; e.s.; FF button; original ribbon (STEIFF printed on ribbon).
CONDITION: Excellent   **PRICE:** $1200-up
(Right) Bunnies. 1905. 2½in (6cm) long; cream velveteen with brown airbrushed spots; black bead eyes; n.j.; cotton stuffing.
CONDITION: Excellent   **PRICE:** $300-up (each)
Private collection.

Rabbits. (Left) Rabbit with Mechanical Head. Circa 1930. 4¾in (12cm); light beige mohair; black tipped ears; glass eyes; unjointed arms and legs; head moves in circular motion by turning tail; e.s.; FF button; red S.L. Rare.
CONDITION: Mint **PRICE:** $1500-up
(Center) Pen Wipe. Circa 1890. 3in (8cm); cream-colored velveteen; airbrush design in brown; red pearl cotton stitched nose and mouth; green felt base with scalloped edge; glass eyes with painted backs; n.j.; k.s. Extremely rare.
CONDITION: Mint **PRICE:** $1200-up
(Back right) Rattle. Circa 1920. 7in (18cm); orange mohair body; white mohair chest and inner ears; glass eyes; unjointed arms and legs; swivel head; e.s. Rattle is encased in tummy. Rare.
CONDITION: Excellent **PRICE:** $800-up
Private collection.

BOTTOM:
(Left to right) *Niki* Rabbit. Circa 1950. 6in (15cm); off-white mohair airbrushed in brown; glass eyes; pink pearl cotton stitched nose outlined in black; f.j.; e.s.; C.T.
CONDITION: Excellent **PRICE:** $195-up
Niki Rabbit. Circa 1950. 10in (25cm); off-white mohair airbrushed in brown; pink felt lined open mouth; glass eyes; pink pearl cotton stitched nose outlined in black; f.j.; e.s.; R.S.B.
CONDITION: Excellent
PRICE: $275-up
German Rabbit. Circa 1914. 11in (28cm); white mohair; blue mohair coat (an integral part of body); shoe-button eyes; jointed arms; unjointed legs; stationary head; e.s. Original shoes. Rare.
CONDITION: Excellent
PRICE: $500-up
Tête Jumeau Doll. Circa 1880. 24in (61cm); bisque head; glass paperweight eyes; closed mouth; jointed composition body; straight wrists; stamped on back of head "Depose TETE JUMEAU 11."
CONDITION: Excellent
PRICE: $6000-up

Hollander Rabbit. Circa 1910. 11in (28cm); white mohair; pink glass eyes; pale tan pearl cotton stitched nose and mouth; f.j.; "moveable ears;" e.s. Rare.
CONDITION: Excellent **PRICE:** $1200-up
Rabbits. Circa 1950. 6in (15cm); 4in (10cm); beige-colored mohair airbrushed in brown; glass eyes; pink pearl cotton stitched noses outlined in black; unjointed legs; swivel heads; e.s.; R.S.B.
CONDITION: Excellent **PRICE:** 6in (15cm) $95-up
4in (10cm) $75-up

Roly-Droly Rabbits. Circa 1926. 5in (13cm); beige tipped with brown mohair; shoe-button eyes; unjointed body; swivel head; e.s.; FF button; red S.L.; red ribbon with bell around neck; pull string with red wooden knob; FF button affixed to knob. Rabbits are attached to red wooden circles. When wooden wheeled frame is pulled, rabbits turn in circular motion. Rare.
CONDITION: Mint   PRICE: $4000-up
Private collection.

(Left) Standing Rabbit. Circa 1928. 5in (13cm); white mohair tipped with orange; glass eyes; unjointed legs; swivel head; e.s.; FF button. Rare color.
CONDITION: Excellent   PRICE: $500-up
(Center) Standing Rabbit. Circa 1928. 10in (25cm); white and faded pink mohair; pink pearl cotton stitched nose outlined in black thread; glass eyes; unjointed legs; swivel head; e.s.; FF button.
CONDITION: Excellent   PRICE: $800-up
(Right) Sitting Rabbit. Circa 1928. 8in (20cm); white mohair tipped with dark brown; pink pearl cotton stitched nose outlined in black; glass eyes; unjointed legs; swivel head; e.s.; FF button.
CONDITION: Excellent   PRICE: $700-up
Private collection.

Rabbits. Circa 1933. 8½in (21cm); short white mohair (areas airbrushed in gold) heads, arms and legs; cotton fabric bodies; glass eyes; jointed legs; unjointed arms; swivel heads; pink pearl cotton stitched nose and mouth; s.s. (stuffed firm); FF button. Dressed as a boy and girl.
CONDITION: Excellent
PRICE: $1200-up (pair)
Private collection.

Rabbits. Circa 1933. (Left) 10½in (26cm); (Right) 8½in (21cm); white mohair head, paws and feet; cotton fabric body; red pearl cotton stitched nose and mouth; glass eyes; unjointed arms and legs; swivel head; e.s.; FF button. Original blue and white cotton pajamas.
CONDITION: Excellent
PRICE: (Left) $2000-up
(Right) $1500-up
Private collection.

Running Rabbit on Eccentric Wheels. Circa 1930. 12in (31cm) long; short blonde mohair; pink pearl cotton stitched nose outlined in black cotton; glass eyes; e.s.; red painted wooden wheels on metal frame. Eccentric wheels give the animal - more natural movement and gait.
CONDITION: Excellent
PRICE: $1200-up
Private collection.

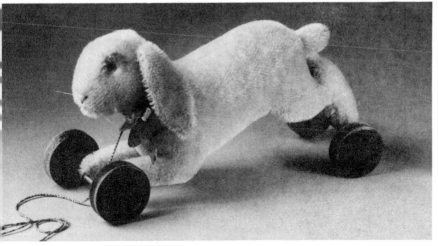

Record Hansi Rabbit. Circa 1955. Approximately 10in (25cm); blonde mohair; glass eyes; pink pearl cotton stitched nose outlined in black cotton; pink felt lined open mouth; f.j.; e.s.; FF button; yellow S.L.
CONDITION: Mint   **PRICE:** $600-up
Private collection.

Fireman Monkey Doll. Circa 1914. 20in (51cm); pale beige mohair head; beige felt face, ears and hands; navy blue felt coat and black felt pants (clothes are integral part of body); leather hat and boots; glass eyes; f.j.; e.s.; FF button. Rare.
CONDITION: Excellent   **PRICE:** $4000-up
Private collection.

Record Peter Monkey. Circa
1920. 10in (25cm); beige felt
face and ears; tan felt head;
beige felt paws; red felt outfit
(suit an integral part of body);
shoe-button eyes; f.j.; e.s.; FF
button.
CONDITION: Mint
PRICE: $1000-up
Private collection.

BELOW:
Chimpanzee (Movable Head
Mechanism). Circa 1933.
Beige mohair tipped with
brown; beige felt face, paws
and feet; glass eyes; f.j.; e.s.
When tail is turned, head will
move in circular motion.
CONDITION: Excellent
PRICE: $1000-up
Private collection.

Mimoccula Orangutang. Circa 1938. 7in (18cm); long reddish-brown mohair; beige felt face, paws and feet; glass eyes ("eyes move" from side to side when ear is pulled); f.j.; e.s.; FF button; red S.L. Rare.
CONDITION: Excellent   **PRICE:** $2000-up
Private collection.

Coco Baboon. Circa 1950. 14in (36cm); long silvery-gray mohair; beige felt face; gray felt paws; glass eyes; f.j.; e.s.; R.S.B. Hat not original.
CONDITION: Excellent   **PRICE:** $350-up
Courtesy Ho Phi Le.

Jocko Monkey. Circa 1950. Dark brown mohair; white mohair chin; beige felt face (painted facial features) ears and paws; glass eyes; f.j.; e.s.; R.S.B.; yellow paper S.L.; C.T.
CONDITION: Mint
PRICE: 10in (25cm) $125-up
               16in (41cm) $225-up
               26in (66cm) $375-up
               30in (76cm) $525-up

(Top row left to right) Monkey. Circa 1950. 30in (76cm); long brown mohair; beige felt face, ears and paws; glass eyes; f.j.; e.s.; R.S.B.
CONDITION: Excellent   **PRICE:** $500-up
Monkey. Circa 1950. 10in (25cm); long brown mohair; beige felt face, ears and paws; glass eyes; f.j.; e.s.; R.S.B.; C.T. reads: "Jocko."
CONDITION: Mint   **PRICE:** $125-up
Monkey. Circa 1950. 18in (46cm); short cinnamon-colored mohair; beige felt face, ears and paws; glass eyes; f.j.; e.s.; R.S.B.; original clothes.
CONDITION: Excellent   **PRICE:** $300-up
Giraffe. Circa 1950. 30in (76cm); short golden-colored mohair with airbrushed orange spots; beige felt lined open mouth and ears; brown mane; glass eyes; n.j.; e.s.
CONDITION: Excellent   **PRICE:** $550-up
(Bottom row left to right) Monkeys (seated together). Circa 1950. 25in (64cm) and 30in (76cm);

long brown mohair; beige felt faces, ears and paws; glass eyes; f.j; e.s.; R.S.B.
25in (64cm)
CONDITION: Excellent   **PRICE:** $375-up
30in (76cm)
CONDITION: Good   **PRICE:** $450-up
Monkey. Circa 1970. 22in (56cm); long brown acrylic plush; beige velveteen face, ears and paws; glass eyes; f.j.; s.s.; I.B.
CONDITION: Excellent   **PRICE:** $200-up
Wurlitzer Band Organ. Circa 1927. 80in (203cm) by 75in (192cm).
CONDITION: Excellent   **PRICE:** $20,000-up
Carmel Carousel Horse. Circa 1920. 50in (128cm) by 48in (122cm).
CONDITION: Excellent   **PRICE:** $8000-up
Hershall Spillman Carousel Horse. Circa 1920. 50in (128cm) by 36in (91cm).
CONDITION: Excellent   **PRICE:** $5000-up

(Left) Wollie Mouse. Circa 1935. 1½in (4cm); white wool; pink glass eyes; pink felt feet; black rubber tail; s.s.; FF button.
CONDITION: Excellent   PRICE: $75-up
(Right) Fluffy Cat. Circa 1926. 8in (20cm); white mohair; tipped with lavender; green glass eyes; pink pearl cotton stitched nose, mouth and claws; stationary legs; swivel head; e.s.; FF button. C.T. reads: "Fluffy."
CONDITION: Excellent   PRICE: $800-up
Private collection.

Kitty. (Movable Head Mechanism). Circa 1935. 10in (25cm); pale beige mohair; green glass eyes; jointed legs; e.s.; FF button. When tail is turned, head will move in circular motion.
CONDITION: Excellent PRICE: $900-up
Private collection.

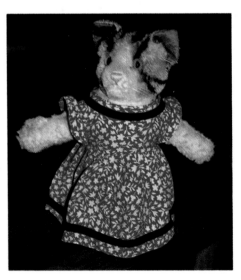

Musical Cat. Circa 1948. 9in (23cm); white mohair with gray and black striped head; white mohair arms and body; green glass eyes; unjointed arms; swivel head; e.s.; cylinder music box is encased in body. Music is produced by pushing downwards in body. Rare.
CONDITION: Excellent   PRICE: $450-up
Courtesy Barbara Baldwin.

Dachshund. Circa
1910. 14in (36cm)
long; black and tan bur-
lap; shoe-button eyes;
f.j.; e.s.; blank button.
CONDITION:
Excellent
PRICE: $800-up
Private collection.

Saint Bernard Dog on
Metal Wheels. Circa
1913. 17in (43cm) tall;
off-white and rust col-
ored mohair; brown
pearl cotton stitched
nose; glass eyes; n.j.;
e.s.; original leather
collar.
CONDITION: Excel-
ent
PRICE: $800-up
Courtesy Barbara
Baldwin.

Fox. Circa 1914. 20in (51cm)
long; tan and white mohair; glass
eyes; f.j.; e.s.; FF button.
CONDITION: Good
PRICE: $800-up
Private collection.

Bonzo Dog. Circa 1927. 12in (31cm); beige velveteen; painted features; red felt tongue; googly glass eyes; f.j.; e.s.; FF button; red S.L.; "white" C.T. Extremely rare.
CONDITION: Excellent
PRICE: $4800-up
Courtesy Barbara Baldwin.

(Left) **Pug-Dog.** Circa 1933. 11in (28cm); long and short blonde, beige and brown mohair head; short blonde mohair arms and feet; cotton fabric body; glass eyes; unjointed arms and legs; swivel head; e.s.; FF button; red S.L.; clothes not original.
CONDITION: Good
PRICE: $500-up
(Right) **Treff** Dog Purse. Circa 1931. 11in (28cm); short tan mohair; glass eyes; unjointed arms and legs; swivel head; e.s. head and legs; red S.L. The body of the dog is lined and the empty cavity serves as the purse. Pictured in Steiff's 1931 catalog only.
CONDITION: Excellent
PRICE: $900-up
Private collection.

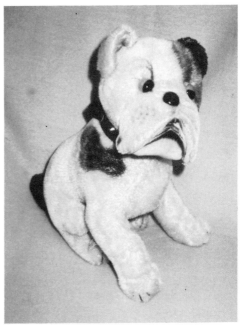

Pip Dog. Circa 1930. 4in (10cm) tall; blue velveteen; beige velveteen in-set snout; red felt tongue; glass googly eyes; unjointed legs; swivel head; FF button; red S.L. Rare.
CONDITION: Mint   PRICE: $575-up
Courtesy Barbara Baldwin.

Bully Dog (College Mascot Series). Seated position. Circa 1950. 12in (31cm); short beige and brown mohair; large glass "googly" eyes; stationary legs; swivel head; e.s.; R.S.B.; U.S. Zone Germany label sewn into seam of body. Rare.
CONDITION: Excellent   PRICE: $850-up
Courtesy Barbara Baldwin.

Loopy Wolf. Circa 1950. 12in (31cm) tall; long and short gray silky mohair; short gray mohair in-set snout; long red felt tongue; beige felt lined mouth; glass eyes; stationary legs; swivel head; e.s.; R.S.B.; C.T. reads "Loopy." Rare.
CONDITION: Mint   PRICE: $1200-up
Courtesy Barbara Baldwin.

Bazi Musical Dog. Circa 1951. 9½in (24cm); reddish-brown mohair head; short blonde mohair chin, body and arms; glass eyes; unjointed arms; swivel head; e.s.; R.S.B.; tube body conceals music box; bellows produces music when tube body is pressed in downward motion. Label sewn into side reads: "Made in U.S. Zone Germany." Originally wore clothes.
CONDITION: Excellent
PRICE: $550-up
Private collection.

BELOW:
Elephant on Wheels. Circa 1926. 14in (36cm) long by 11in (28cm) tall; charcoal gray mohair; white felt tusks; blue glass eyes; n.j.; FF button; e.s. Metal frame with red painted wooden wheels. Original blue mohair blanket and head dress trimmed in red fringe. Produced from 1926 to 1928.
CONDITION: Excellent
PRICE: $2000-up
Private collection.

(Left) Elephant Doll. Circa
1935. 11in (28cm); short gray
mohair head and paws; cotton
fabric body; blue glass eyes;
unjointed arms and legs;
swivel head; e.s.; FF button;
original clothes.
CONDITION: Excellent
PRICE: $1500-up
(Right) Elephant. Circa 1910.
Gray mohair; shoe-button
eyes; f.j.; e.s.; FF button.
CONDITION: Excellent
PRICE: $800-up
Wooden Blocks. Circa 1938.
CONDITION: Good
PRICE: $250-up
Private collection.

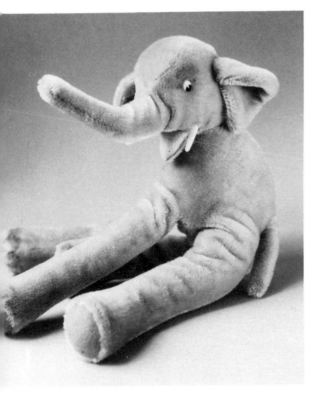

Dangly Elephant. Circa 1950.
14in (36cm); short gray mohair; glass eyes; beige felt lined
open mouth; unjointed arms
and legs; swivel head; e.s.;
R.S.B.
CONDITION: Excellent
PRICE: $750-up
Private collection.

(Left) Duckling. Circa 1938. 4in (10cm); blonde "wool" plush; orange felt beak and feet; black glass eyes; n.j.; e.s.; FF button.
CONDITION: Good   **PRICE:** $150-up
(Center left) Duckling. Circa 1935. 6in (15cm); yellow "wool" plush; orange felt beak and feet; black glass eyes; n.j.; e.s.; FF button.
CONDITION: Good   **PRICE:** $250-up
(Center right) Duck Doll. Circa 1933. 11in (28cm); pale yellow mohair head, paws and feet; cotton fabric body; orange felt beak; shoe-button eyes; unjointed arms and legs; swivel head; e.s.; FF button; original bathing suit.
CONDITION: Good   **PRICE:** $800-up
(Right) Duckling. Circa 1935. 6in (15cm); white "wool" plush; orange felt beak and feet; black glass eyes; n.j.; e.s.
CONDITION: Good   **PRICE:** $250-up
Private collection.

(Left) Duck (Movable Head Mechanism). Circa 1933. 8in (20cm); short green, gold and pale yellow mohair; orange felt beak and feet; black glass eyes; unjointed legs; e.s.; FF button. When tail is turned, head will move in circular motion.
CONDITION: Excellent   **PRICE:** $750-up
(Center) Duck. Circa 1926. 5in (13cm); short green, gold and yellow mohair; orange felt beak and feet; black glass eyes; n.j.; e.s.; FF button.
CONDITION: Excellent   **PRICE:** $300-up
(Right) Comic Duck. Circa 1928. 6in (15cm); orange and faded yellow (originally blue) mohair; red felt beak and feet; black and white glass googly eyes; n.j.; e.s.; FF button.
CONDITION: Good   **PRICE:** $500-up
Private collection.

(Left) Chick. Circa 1925. 3in (8cm); white
mohair; yellow felt beak and feet; shoe-
button eyes; n.j.; e.s.; FF button.
CONDITION: Excellent
PRICE: $200-up
(Right) Hen Egg Warmers. Circa 1912.
4in (10in); white and red felt; FF button.
CONDITION: Excellent
PRICE: $150-up each
Private collection.

Comic Hen. Circa 1928. 9in (23cm); pale
yellow, gold and green mohair; red felt
face; shoe-button eyes backed with white
felt; n.j.; e.s.; FF button.
CONDITION: Excellent
PRICE: $750-up
Private collection.

Possum. Circa 1909. 7in (18cm);
white mohair; shoe-button eyes;
red pearl cotton nose, mouth and
claws; f.j.; e.s.; FF button. Rare,
especially in this size.
CONDITION: Good
PRICE: $2000-up
Billy Possum Fork. Circa 1909.
6in (15cm); coin silver plate;
front embossed "Billie Possum."
CONDITION: Excellent
PRICE: $70-up
Crite postcard. Circa 1909. Billie
Possum is about to devour the
"Special meal for the day" —
"Roast Teddy Bear."
CONDITION: Mint
PRICE: $50-up
Private collection.

(Left) Possum. Circa 1909. 12in (31cm) long; light honey-colored mohair tipped with brown; shoe-button eyes; f.j.; swivel tail; e.s.; FF button. Rare.
CONDITION: Mint   PRICE: $3500-up
(Right) Steiff Pig. Movable Head. Circa 1914. 5in (13cm) tall; white mohair; shoe-button eyes; jointed legs; ball-jointed neck; movable head (head moves in circular motion); e.s.; FF button; remnant white S.L.
CONDITION: Excellent   PRICE: $1050-up
Courtesy Patricia Volpe.

(Left) Pig. Circa 1912. 4in (10cm) tall; pink velvet; small shoe-button eyes; red stitched nose and mouth; n.j.; e.s.; FF button.
CONDITION: Excellent   PRICE: $600-up
(Center) Pig. Circa 1928. 6in (15cm) tall; white mohair; glass eyes; n.j.; e.s.; FF button; red S.L.; two-colored ruff.
CONDITION: Excellent   PRICE: $1000-up
(Right) Pig. Movable Head. Circa 1914. 6in (15cm) tall; blonde mohair; shoe-button eyes; jointed legs; ball-jointed neck; movable head (head moves in circular motion); e.s.; FF button
CONDITION: Excellent   PRICE: $1000-up
Private collection.

Lamb on Wheels. Circa 1900. 23in (58cm) long by 20in (51cm) tall; white curly wool; beige felt face and legs; glass eyes; n.j.; e.s.; iron frame and wheels; pull cry box. Rare.

CONDITION: Excellent *Courtesy Denise Grey.*

PRICE: $3000-up

Sheep on Wheels. Circa 1938. 14in (36cm); off-white curly wool; short beige mohair in-set snout; ears and base of legs; leather hooves; glass eyes; n.j.; e.s.; blue painted wooden wheels; FF button.
CONDITION: Good
PRICE: $600-up
Private collection.

Horse on Wheels. Pull Toy. Circa 1908. 20in (51cm) tall; reddish-brown and beige felt; glass eyes; n.j.; e.s.; FF button; black horse hair mane and tail; felt blanket; leather saddle, bridle and harness; metal wheels; frame and handle; handle crosses over horse to pull.
CONDITION: Mint
PRICE: $2600-up
Circa 1910. 13in (33cm); gold mohair; shoe-button eyes; f.j.; e.s.; FF button.
CONDITION: Excellent
PRICE: $1300-up
Courtesy Barbara Baldwin.

BELOW:
(Left) Horse on Wheels. Circa 1920. 10in (25cm); reddish-brown and cream-colored felt; glass eyes; n.j.; e.s.; FF button; wooden wheels on metal frame; leather saddle.
CONDITION: Excellent
PRICE: $600-up
(Right) Donkey on Wheels. Circa 1913. 8in (20cm); gray mohair; shoe-button eyes; n.j.; e.s.; FF button; metal wheels on metal frame; leather saddle.
CONDITION: Good
PRICE: $700-up
Private collection.

Lion (College Mascot Series). Circa 1948. 18in (46cm); gold mohair; long reddish-brown mohair mane; red pearl cotton stitched nose outlined in black cotton; glass "googly" eyes; n.j.; e.s. Label sewn into seam of body reads "U.S. Zone Germany." Rare.
CONDITION: Excellent   **PRICE:** $800-up
Private collection.

This illustration is a representation of Steiff animals from the 1950s ranging in size from 5in (13cm) to 9in (23cm). Animals (left to right) Robby the seal, Goose and gosling, duckling, Whittie the owl, doe, Flossy the fish, fox, and Raccy the raccoon.
CONDITION: Excellent   **PRICE:** Ranges from $95 to $300-up

BELOW:
Animated Display. Circa 1948. 21ft (640cm) by 7ft (213cm). Numerous Steiff animals come to life in an amusing setting, driven by electric motors. Rare.
CONDITION: Good   **PRICE:** $20,000-up

Nelly Snails. Circa 1950. 4in (10cm); green and brown velveteen; plastic shells and antennae; glass eyes; e.s.; R.S.B.; yellow S.L.; C.T. Rare.
CONDITION: Mint
PRICE: $275-up (each)
Courtesy Barbara Baldwin.

Hedgehogs. (Left) Micki; (Right) Mecki. Circa 1950. 10in (25cm); rubber faces; painted facial features; brown hair tipped with white; felt bodies; f.j.; e.s.; R.S.B.
CONDITION: Excellent
PRICE: $90-up (each)

BELOW:
Birds with Movable Wings. Circa 1958. 4¼in (11cm); various colors of mohair; dyed horsehair wings; glass eyes; n.j.; e.s.; R.S.B.; yellow S.L.; C.T. Squeezing legs together activates wing movement.
CONDITION: Mint
PRICE: $275-up
Courtesy Barbara Baldwin.

Tags, Buttons and Labels Used by Steiff
from 1900 to Present Day

The famous Steiff trademark, a small nickel button embedded in the toy animal's left ear was first used in 1904 and officially registered the next year.

Paper chest tag (drawing of tag) used from 1900 to 1903/4.

Paper chest tag used from 1928 to 1950. From 1984 used for the replica series of bears and animals from 1928 until 1950.

White paper chest tag with metal edge used from 1926 to 1928. From 1983 white tag used for the replica series for animals and bears pre-1928.

Paper chest tag used from 1950 to 1972. From 1983 used for replica series of bears and animals from 1950 until 1960s.

Paper chest tag used from 1972 to present day.

1904-1905. Elephant button. An elephant with curved trunk was embossed on a metal button with two prong attachment.

1904/05. Blank button (with first stock label). Small metal blank button with two prong atachment.

1905-1948. Printed (raised) STEIFF button with F underscored on metal button with two prong attachment.

1948-1950. Blank blue painted button (grays with age).

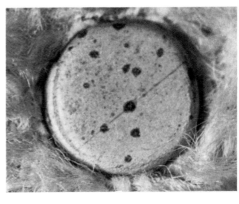

Circa 1950. Printed (raised) STEIFF button without F underscored on metal button with two prong attachment.

1950-1969/70. Raised *Steiff* in script on metal button with two prong attachment.

1970-1978/79. Incised *Steiff* in script on chrome button, riveted in ear.

Circa 1977-1981. Raised *Steiff* in script on brass button, riveted in ear.

1980-present day. Brass button (slightly larger in size to earlier buttons) with incised *Steiff* in script; riveted into ear.

irca 1908 white paper (a special paper oven with fibers on all paper labels); L. Number indicates the exact look of e animal as to posture covering and eight (in centimeters).

irca 1908-1925/26. White paper S.L. lore information added to label geschutzt" (protected by law); Germany nporte d'Allemage (made in Germany).

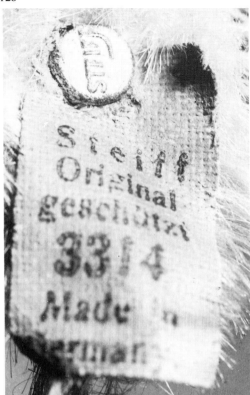

Circa 1925-1934/5. Red stock paper label.

Circa 1935-1950. Yellow stock paper label

Circa 1950-1972. Yellow coated linen label. Note style of information has changed and a place is designated for price.

Circa 1968-1980. Yellow coated linen label. Style of information is the same but a slash is now used instead of a comma.

This design of S.L. was introduced in 1980 and is still used to date. However, the material has changed over the years.

1980-1982. White woven S.L. used for Limited editions.

1980-1982. Yellow woven S.L.

1982-1987. White cloth-weave S.L. used for Limited editions.

1982-1987. Yellow cloth-weave S.L.

1986-Present day. White printed ribbon S.L. used for limited editions.

1986-Present day. Yellow printed ribbon S.L.

STEIFF MUSEUM REPLICAS, SPECIAL AND LIMITED EDITIONS

ITEM No.	YEAR INTRODUCED	NAME	ORIGINAL SUGGESTED RETAIL PRICE	1993 PRICE
0153,43	1980	**PAPA JUBILEE BEAR** Replica 1903, limited to 11,000, boxed, white S.L., certificate.	$150	$825-up
0155,38	1981	**MAMA AND BABY BEAR SET** Replica 1903, limited to 8000, boxed, white S.L., certificate.	$150	$550-up
0150,32	1982	**RICHARD STEIFF BEAR** Replica 1905, limited to 20,000, boxed, white S.L.	$90	$325-up
0203,00	1982	**ORIGINAL TEDDY WHITE SET** Limited 2000, boxed, white S.L..	$300	$400-up
0204,17	1982	**TEA PARTY SET** Four bears boxed, white S.L., certificate, limited to 10,000.	$175	$350-up
0223,30	1982	**BRUNO BEAR** Yellow S.L..	$60	$130-up
0155,26	1982	MARGARET STRONG GOLD BEAR	$48	$120-up
0155,32	1982	MARGARET STRONG GOLD BEAR	$62	$159-up
0155,42	1983	MARGARET STRONG GOLD BEAR	$90	$215-up
0155,51	1984	MARGARET STRONG GOLD BEAR	$185	$385-up
0155,60	1984	MARGARET STRONG GOLD BEAR Yellow S.L. bear, still available.	$250	$589-up
0210,22	1983	**TEDDY ROOSEVELT COMMEMORATIVE SET** Also called the Nimrod Set or Campfire Set, Limited to 10,000, three bears boxed, white S.L., certificate.	$199	$300-up
0165,28	1984	1909 REPLICA GOLD BEAR	$55	$85-up
0165,38	1983	1909 REPLICA GOLD BEAR	$79	$145-up
0165,51	1984	1909 REPLICA GOLD BEAR	$150	$450-up
0165,60	1985	1909 REPLICA GOLD BEAR Open stock, yellow S.L.	$275	$650-up
0160,00	1983	**MARGARET STRONG BEARS CHOCOLATE SET** Replica 1904. Limited to 2000 sets. Bears in set: 7in (18cm); 10in (26cm); 12in (32cm); 16in (42cm)	$275	$550-up
0310,19	1983	**"MANSCHLI" BUDDHA BEAR**	$40	$165-up

ITEM No.	YEAR INTRODUCED	NAME	ORIGINAL SUGGESTED RETAIL PRICE	1993 PRICE
3020,00	1983	**MANNI RABBIT SET** Three standing/begging rabbits set. Limited to 2000. Rabbit sizes are: 4in (10cm), 8in (20cm), and 12in (30cm).	$150	$240-up
0135,00	1984	**HOPPY RABBIT SET** Three running rabbits in this set. Limited to 2000 sets. Rabbit sizes are: 3in (8cm), 6in (14cm), and 7in (17cm).	$150	$200-up
0156,00	1984	**MARGARET STRONG BEAR CINNAMON SET** Replica 1904. Limited to 2000 sets; white S.L. Bears in set: 7in (18cm), 10in (26cm), 12in (32cm), 16in (42cm)	$300	$650-up
0082,20	1984	**ROLY-POLY CIRCUS BEAR** Museum series; replica 1892; limited to 9000; boxed; button only.	$69	$120-up
0080,08	1984	**FELT ELEPHANT** Museum series; replica 1880; limited to 10,000; boxed; button only.	$60	$60-up
0162,00	1984	**GIENGEN TEDDY BEAR SET (MAMA & BABY BEAR)** Limited to 16,000; boxed; white S.L. Mama is 14in (35cm); Baby is 4in (10cm).	$150	$275-up
0151,25	1984	MR. CINNAMON BEAR Replica 1903	$70	$200-up
0151,32	1984	MR. CINNAMON BEAR Replica 1903	$85	$300-up
0151,40	1984	MR. CINNAMON BEAR Replica 1903; yellow S.L.	$125	$500-up
4003	1984	**GOLDILOCKS AND THE THREE BEARS** Limited to 2000 sets, Goldilocks is a Susan Gibson doll, bears are Steiff bears. Papa is 13in (33cm), Mama is 12in (31cm), and Baby is 9½in (24cm). Set is boxed and numbered.	$200	$600-up
0157,26	1984	MARGARET STRONG BEAR (CREAM)	$50	$130-up
0157,32	1984	MARGARET STRONG BEAR (CREAM)	$65	$200-up
0157,42	1984	MARGARET STRONG BEAR (CREAM)	$95	$275-up
0157,51	1985	MARGARET STRONG BEAR (CREAM)	$195	$600-up
0157,60	1985	MARGARET STRONG BEAR (CREAM) Replica 1904 bear, yellow S.L.. The 23½in (60cm) size - less than 1000 pieces were made.	$285	$950-up

ITEM No.	YEAR INTRODUCED	NAME	ORIGINAL SUGGESTED RETAIL PRICE	1993 PRICE
0225,42	1984	**OPHELIA BEAR** Boxed; button only.	$150	$325-up
0227,27	1988	**BABY OPHELIA BEAR** Button only.	$140	$175-up
0134,22	1984	NIKI RABBIT Replica 1952. Limited to 3500; white S.L..	$58	$175-up
0134,28	1984	NIKI RABBIT Replica 1952. Limited to 2500; white S.L.	$70	$200-up
4004	1985	**GOLDILOCKS AND THE THREE BEARS** This is the smaller of the two sets. Limited to 5000. Papa is 9in (23cm), Mama is 7in (18cm), Baby is 5in (13cm); white S.L.	$300	$350-up
0172,32	1985	**DICKY BEAR** Replica 1930. Limited to 20,000; boxed; white S.L.; certificate.	$99.50	$275-up
0167,22	1986	GIENGEN BEAR GREY	$55	$120-up
0167,32	1985	GIENGEN BEAR GREY	$85	$175-up
0167,42	1985	GIENGEN BEAR GREY	$120	$350-up
0167,52	1986	GIENGEN BEAR GREY Replica 1906; yellow S.L.	$195	$495-up
0245,40	1985	**PASSPORT BEAR** Comes with a passport which can be validated!! Yellow S.L.	$110	$225-up
0251,34	1985	**BERLIN BEAR** Boxed; yellow S.L.	$110	$215-up
0085,12	1985	**BEAR ON WHEELS** Replica 1905. Museum series; limited to 12,000; boxed; button only.	$95	$155-up
0105,17	1985	**PENGUIN** Replica 1928. Museum series. Limited to 8000; boxed; button only.	$75	$150-up
0211,26	1985	LUV BEAR	$45	$130-up
0211,36	1985	LUV BEAR	$60	$160-up
0155,37	1984	M. STRONG BEAR BRIDE	$100	$250-up
0155,36	1984	M. STRONG BEAR GROOM	$100	$250-up
0155,22	1985	M. STRONG BEAR FLOWER BEAR-ER	$75	$150-up
0155,23	1985	M. STRONG BEAR RING BEAR-ER	$75	$150-up
0155,34	1986	M. STRONG BEAR VICTORIAN GIRL	$125	$200-up
0155,35	1986	M. STRONG BEAR VICTORIAN BOY	$125	$200-up

ITEM No.	YEAR INTRODUCED	NAME	ORIGINAL SUGGESTED RETAIL PRICE	1993 PRICE
0156,36	1987	M. STRONG BEAR VICTORIAN LADY	$150	$200-up
0156,37	1987	M. STRONG BEAR VICTORIAN MAN	$150	$200-up
0155,15	1986	M. STRONG CHRISTENING BEAR	$60	$150-up
0156,34	1988	M. STRONG BEAR "CAPTAIN STRONG"	$200	$250-up
0155,22e	1988	M. STRONG ELF BEAR	$99	$130-up
0155,22	1988	M. STRONG ELF BEAR - UNDRESSED	N/A	$100-up
0155,38	1986	M. STRONG SANTA	$125	$250-up
0156,38	1987	M. STRONG VICTORIAN SANTA BEAR Margaret Strong Dressed Bears; Replica 1904 yellow S.L.; boxed (except for the elf bears).	$150	$250-up
0158,25	1985	MARGARET STRONG WHITE W/LEATHER PAWS	$60	$200-up
0158,31	1985	MARGARET STRONG WHITE W/LEATHER PAWS	$79	$300-up
0158,41	1985	MARGARET STRONG WHITE W/LEATHER PAWS	$110	$400-up
0158,50	1986	MARGARET STRONG WHITE W/LEATHER PAWS Replica 1904 Bear. 20in (50cm) is limited to only 750. Other three sizes are limited to 2000. White S.L.	$225	$1500-up
0170,32	1986	**TEDDY CLOWN** Replica 1926. Limited to 10,000; boxed; white S.L.; certificate.	$150	$345-up
0168,22	1986	GIENGEN BEAR (GOLD)	$55	$150-up
0168,42	1986	GIENGEN BEAR (GOLD) Replica 1906; yellow S.L.	$125	$295-up
0101,14	1986	**BULLY DOG** Replica 1927. Museum series; button only; boxed.	$75	$125-up
0100,86	1986	ELEPHANT AND CALLIOPE	$299	
0100,87	1987	LION/CAGE	$275	
0100,88	1988	GIRAFFE/CAGE	$325	$2220-up (set)
0100,89	1989	TIGER/CAGE	$350	
0100,90	1990	BEAR/CAGE	$450	
0163,19	1987	**TEDDY CLOWN JR.** Replica 1905. Limited to 5000. 2000 w/ yellow S.L., 3000 with white S.L.	$50	$175-up
0164,31	1987	CIRCUS DOLLY BEAR (YELLOW)	$135	$200-up
0164,32	1987	CIRCUS DOLLY BEAR (GREEN)	$135	$200-up
0164,33	1987	CIRCUS DOLLY BEAR (VIOLET) Replica 1913, limited to 2000 each, white S.L.	$135	$200-up

ITEM No.	YEAR INTRODUCED	NAME	ORIGINAL SUGGESTED RETAIL PRICE	1993 PRICE
0164,30	1987	CIRCUS DOLLY BEAR (PALE YELLOW)	$185	$295-up
0120,10	1988	BEAR BANDSMAN	$125	$165-up
0121,19	1988	DOG BANDSMAN	$125	$135-up
0122,19	1988	CAT BANDSMAN	$125	$135-up
0123,19	1988	LION BANDSMAN	$125	$135-up
0124,19	1988	CROCODILE BANDSMAN Limited to 5000 each.	$125	$135-up
0163,20	1989	**CLOWN TEDDY** Replica 1909. Limited to 5000, white clown, numbered on C.T.	$99	$130-up
0175,19	1989	TEDDY BABY RINGMASTER	$140	$170-up
0146,19	1989	HIPPO FAT LADY	$135	$135-up
0147,12	1989	SEAL WITH BALL ON STAND	$100	$135-up
0145,19	1989	BABY ELEPHANT BALLOON SELLER	$135	$135-up
0143,19	1989	CHIMP ON UNICYCLE Teddy Baby limited to 7000 pieces. All other pieces are limited to 5000. White S.L.	$125	$165-up
0190,35	1988	JACKIE BEAR - limited to 4000	$300	$300-up
0190,25	1987	JACKIE BEAR - limited to 10,000	$135	$175-up
0190,17	1989	JACKIE BEAR - limited to 12,000 Replica 1953.	$135	$145-up
1071,41	1987	TEDDY ROSE BEAR Limited to 10,000	$200	$325-up
0171,25	1990	TEDDY ROSE BEAR Limited to 8000 Replica 1925, boxed, white S.L. certificate.	$195	$225-up
0211,10	1990	TEDDY ROSE BEAR Open stock, yellow S.L.	$59	$70-up
0104,19	1986	**TABBY CAT** Replica 1928. Museum series; limited to 6000; boxed; button only.	$75	$125-up
0227,33	1987	**SCHNUFFY** Replica 1907 Boxed; button only.	$199	$300-up
0090,11	1987	**POLAR BEAR** Replica 1909. Museum series; limited to 3600; button only.	$95	$240-up
0131,00	1987	**THREE BEARS IN A TUB** Butcher, baker and candlestick maker all come in a wooden tub. Limited to 1800; white S.L.	$275	$350-up
0225,35	1987	**CLIFFORD BERRYMAN BEAR** Yellow S.L.	$169	$250-up

ITEM No.	YEAR INTRODUCED	NAME	ORIGINAL SUGGESTED RETAIL PRICE	1993 PRICE
0207,26		ORIGINAL TEDDY - GREY	$45	$65-up
0207,41		ORIGINAL TEDDY - GREY	$62	$125-up
0155,18	1988	ROLY POLY BEAR Replica 1908.	$125	$140-up
0174,35	1990	MUZZLE BEAR (WHITE) Limited to 6000	$295	$295-up
0174,46	1988	MUZZLE BEAR (WHITE) Limited to 5000	$375	$375-up
0174,60	1989	MUZZLE BEAR (WHITE) Limited to 2650 Replica 1908. White S.L.	$500	$525-up
0173,40	1988	**BLACK BEAR** Replica 1907. Limited to 4000; white S.L.; boxed, certificate.	$300	$500-up
0095,17	1988	**HOLLÄNDER RABBIT** Replica 1911. Museum series; limited to 4000; boxed; button only. Rabbit is seven way jointed.	$145	$150-up
0132,24	1988	**"WIGWAG" BEAR PULL TOY** Replica 1924; museum series; limited to 4000; boxed; white S.L.	$260	$260-up
0130,28	1989	**BEAR ON ALL FOURS** Replica 1931; limited to 4000, white S.L.; boxed; certificate. Bear turns head by turning tail.	$400	$450-up
0135,20	1989	**BABY BEAR PULL TOY** Prototype 1939. Museum series; limited to 4000; white S.L.; boxed.	$275	$275-up
0180,50	1989	**PETSY BEAR (BI-COLOR, BLUE EYES)** Replica 1927; limited to 5000; white S.L.; boxed; certificate.	$375	$435-up
0181,35	1989	**PETSY BEAR (BRASS-COLOR)** Replica 1927. Limited to 5000; white S.L.; boxed; certificate.	$225	$285-up
0164,29	1990	**SOMERSAULT BEAR** Replica 1909. Limited to 5000 pieces. This unique bear will do somerssaults by winding his arm. Boxed; white S.L.; certificate.	$395	$395-up
0188,25	1990	**BEAR WITH NECK MECHANISM** Bear moves his head by turning his tail. Replica 1955 Limited to 4000 pieces. Boxed; white S.L.; certificate.	$200	$250-up

ITEM No.	YEAR INTRODUCED	NAME	ORIGINAL SUGGESTED RETAIL PRICE	1993 PRICE
0169,65	1990	**BICOLOR BEAR** Replica 1926. Limited to 5000, boxed, white S.L. certificate.	$525	$600-up
0169,40	1991	**BICOLOR BEAR** 1926 Replica Limited to 6000, boxed, white S.L.; certificate	$375	$395-up
0116,25	1990	**RECORD TEDDY** Replica 1913. Museum series. Limited to 4000.	$300	$350-up
0150,50 EAN NO. 404108	1991	**35PB "BAERLE" BEAR** Replica 1903; limited to 6000; boxed; white S.L.	$795	$795-up
0243,32	1988	**WALT DISNEY WORLD 1ST CONVENTION** Honey-colored Margaret Strong Bear w/ suede paws. Limited to 1000.	$99	$350-up
0244,35	1989	**WALT DISNEY WORLD 2ND CONVENTION** White Petsy Bear. Limited to 1000.	$150	$300-up
0245,32	1990	**WALT DISNEY WORLD 3RD CONVENTION** Charcoal grey bear, limited to 1000.	$125	$275-up
	1991	**WALT DISNEY WORLD 4TH CONVENTION** Black Margaret Strong, limited to 1500. Bear has a Mickey Mouse Mask also.	$175	$275-up
0174,61	1989	**1907 ENGLISH TEDDY** Limited to 2000	N/A	$800-up
0174,33	1990	**1906 ENGLISH SCHNUFFY** Limited to 3000	N/A	$325-up
0173,48	1991	**1912 BLACK TEDDY** - limited to 3000	N/A	$500-up
0184,35	1990	**"ALFONSO"** - Made for "Teddy Bears of Whitney" Limited to 5000.	$300	$300-up
0177,00	1988	**TEDDY BABY & WOLF SET** Limited to 1000. Made for a toy store in Germany.	N/A	$650-up
0168,28	1989	**1906 REPLICA MADE FOR HAMLEY'S** Limited to 1000.	N/A	$185-up
	1991	**RALPH LAUREN POLO BEAR** Limited to 250; yellow S.L. 1909 Blond dressed.	N/A	$550-up

Note: Items discontinued unless otherwise noted.

Unidentified German Manufactured Bears

Circa 1915. 17in (43cm); blonde-colored mohair; large glass eyes; f.j.; e.s.
CONDITION: Excellent   PRICE: $1200-up
Private collection.

Circa 1920. 6in (15cm) and 4in (10cm); sparse short bright gold bristle-type mohair; glass stickpin eyes; wire jointed arms and legs; stationary head; e.s. Marked "Germany" on blue paper ribbon around neck.
CONDITION: Excellent
PRICE: 6in (15cm) $95-up
       4in (10cm) $50-up
Courtesy Marge Adolphson.

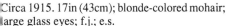

Circa 1915. 11in (28cm); white mohair (grayed with age); papier-mâché head is covered with mohair; carved wooden open mouth with painted teeth; glass sleep eyes; pink wax eyelids; black "glass" nose; f.j.; e.s.; tilt type growler. Rare. Note the resemblance to the Peter Bear (page 58).
CONDITION: Good   PRICE: $2800-up
Courtesy Nancy Permakoff.

Clown Bear. Circa 1920. 12in (31cm); short gold mohair head and paws; cotton twill body; glass eyes; n.j.; wire armature encased in arms; original cotton clown outfit, felt hat and shoes; e.s. Original box. Printed on box "PECO, Ges Geschutzt."
CONDITION: Mint
PRICE: $600-up
Courtesy Lawrence Kindler.

Unidentified German Manufacturer. "Jester" Bear. Circa 1908. 33in (84cm); pale gold mohair; glass eyes; sealing wax nose; f.j.; e.s.; gold and blue wool plush jester costume and integral part of body; cream and orange felt ruff decorated with brass bells; cream felt cuffs. Very rare.
CONDITION: Excellent
PRICE: Sold at Christie's November 1991
            auction for £3300 (approximately
            $6300).
Courtesy Christie's Kensington, England.

Circa 1935. 20in (51cm); gold cotton plush; glass eyes;
f.j.; e.s.
CONDITION: Excellent   **PRICE:** $350-up (each)
Courtesy Brigitte Nohrudi.

Pustefix Bubble Blowing Bear. 1992. 32in
(81cm); brown mohair; short mohair in-set
snout; felt lined open mouth; electric bubble
blowing mechanism concealed in stomach;
f.j.; s.s. Used as a display piece to promote
the company's bubble blowing product.
Action: Arm moves down into bubble blowing solution and up to mouth to blow bubbles.
CONDITION: Mint   **PRICE:** $800-up
Courtesy Pustefix.

CHAPTER 4

BEARS AND SOFT TOYS OF VARIOUS ORIGIN

(Australian, Austrian, French, Polish, Swiss and Japanese)

Australian Bears

The first Australian Bear is thought to have been made by Joy-Toys in the 1920s. This company struggled along until 1937 when it began to produce Walt Disney characters. Although the company flourished with 150 different kinds of toys, the teddy bear was the most desirable with nearly 50,000 sold while in business.

Early Joy-Toys were mohair and fully jointed. Later, only the limbs were jointed. The head was stationary. Noses were very distinctive with black woolen thread stitched vertically with the outside stitches elongated upwards. Bears were mainly identified with a Joy-Toys label on the left foot.

Over the years, the company was forced to use lower quality materials. After changing hands several times, the name was last used in 1976.

Lindee Toy made bears between the 1930s to 1970s, but little is known about these Australian collectibles.

Verna is another well-known Australian teddy bear maker. Still in business, Verna bears are identified by a square-shaped snout. At one time these bears were made of fine mohair and were fully jointed. Now the company produces bears with synthetic fur in both jointed and un-jointed versions.

A quartet of notable Australian bear manufacturers which emulate the British style of teddy bears are Berlex Toys, Jakas, Emile and Parker Toys.

Berlex Pandas. Circa 1950. 18in (46cm); black and white cotton plush; vinyl paw pads; glass eyes; jointed arms and legs; stationary heads; s.s.
CONDITION: Excellent
PRICE: $300-up (each)
Courtesy Romy Roeder.

Verna Bear. Circa 1950. 30in (76cm); gold-colored mohair; vinyl paw pads; plastic eyes; f.j.; black felt nose (typical of Verna bears); foam rubber stuffing.
CONDITION: Excellent
PRICE: $600-up
Courtesy Romy Roeder.

Joy Toys' Bear. Circa 1930. 24in (61cm); gold-colored mohair; glass eyes; f.j.; nose vertically stitched in black wool with two outer stitches elongated upwards; e.s. head; s.s. body.
CONDITION: Excellent
PRICE: $600-up
Courtesy Romy Roeder.

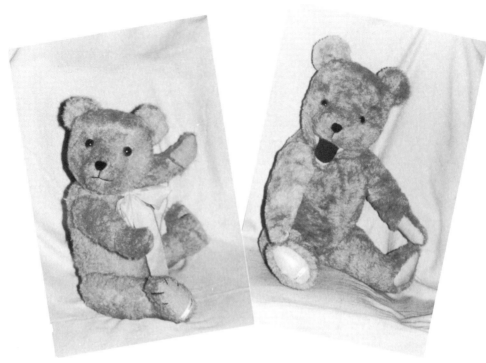

(Left) **Jakas** Bear. Circa 1950. 15in (38cm); gold-colored mohair; glass eyes; f.j.; foam rubber stuffing; label on foot reads: "Jakas Toys."
CONDITION: Excellent   **PRICE:** $250-up
(Right) **Jakas** Bear. Circa 1950. 15in (38cm)

caramel-colored wool blend; plastic eyes; f.j.; vinyl paw pads; foam rubber stuffing; label on foot reads: "Jakas Toys".
CONDITION: Excellent   **PRICE:** $350-up
Courtesy Romy Roeder.

Berg Bears of Austria

Once again, old U.S. Army blankets and buttons from old uniforms were put to good use after World War II. By 1951, the enterprising Berg Brothers purchased real woven plush and life-like glass eyes.

At first Berg bears were identified by a small white tag affixed to the ear. After exhibiting at the famous Nurnberg Toy Fair, these toys wore little red hearts around their necks and were called "animals with a heart."

Circa 1970. 5in (13cm); short pale beige mohair; plastic eyes; f.j.; e.s.; red heart attached to chest reads: "Tiere mit Herz" (animal with heart). Early Berg bears were identified with a label and later a green embossed button.
CONDITION: Excellent   **PRICE:** $60-up

Fechter Bears of Austria

The first Fechter bears were sewn from American army green towels by a former teddy bear seamstress from Central Germany. While Berta Fechter (nee Bohn) hand-sewed bears, her husband cut joints individually with a pocketknife. By the Vienna Toy Fair of 1950 more than 20 factory workers were employed.

Fechter bears are recognizable by their shield-shaped, embroidered nose with a downward crescent at the top, the large erect ears with a contrasting lining, the red felt tongue in open mouth models and the absence of air brushing.

Identical pattern bears still can have different fur lengths, muzzle colors and either felt or sheared mohair pads.

The early label read "Fechter Styria." Later examples were either pale yellow satin imprinted with "Fechter Spielwarren" or beige taffeta with "Fechter Rein Mohair" woven in brown. All used an insignia of a bear on the back.

(Left) Circa 1950. 16in (41cm); short gold mohair; glass eyes; f.j.; e.s.
CONDITION: Mint   PRICE: $350-up
(Center) Circa 1960. 14in (36cm); pinkish beige mohair; cream-colored mohair lined ears; glass eyes; f.j.; e.s. Label sewn into outer edge of right ear reads: "Fechter Spielwaren."
CONDITION: Mint   PRICE: $250-up
(Right) Circa 1950. 19in (48cm); tan-colored mohair; cream-colored mohair lined ears; glass eyes; f.j.; e.s.; label sewn into the outer edge of left ear (97% of Fechter bears have tags sewn into the outer edge of right ear).
CONDITION: Mint   PRICE: $475-up
Courtesy N. & C. Bisbikis, Jr.

(Left front) Circa 1950. 14in (36cm); silky bright blue mohair; white mohair in-set snout, ears, tops of paws and feet ("cuffs"); felt lined open mouth; felt paw pads; reddish glass eyes; f.j.; e.s.; label sewn into outer edge of left ear reads: "Fechter Spielwaren."
CONDITION: Mint   PRICE: $350-up
(Left back) Circa 1960. 14in (36cm); gray mohair; white mohair chest; short tan plush in-set snout, paw pads and lining of ears; felt lined open mouth; glass eyes; f.j.; e.s.; label sewn into outer edge of right ear reads: "Fechter Spielwaren."
CONDITION: Mint   PRICE: $325-up
(Right back) Circa 1965. 14in (36cm); white mohair tipped with dark brown; gold mohair chest, in-set snout, paw pads and lining of ears; felt lined open mouth; glass eyes; f.j.; e.s.
CONDITION: Mint   PRICE: $325-up
(Right front) Circa 1955. 13in (33cm); pale tan-colored mohair; white mohair chest; in-set snout, paw pads and lining of ears; felt lined open mouth; glass eyes; f.j.; e.s.
CONDITION: Mint   PRICE: $325-up
Courtesy N. & C. Bisbikis, Jr.

Unidentified French Manufactured Bears

Prosper. Circa 1934. 13in (33cm); white painted composition swivel head; original chain attached to nose; white mohair (worn) jointed arms; stationary legs; black formed cotton fabric shoes; e.s.; black velvet outfit. Rare. Prosper is from the French comic strip drawn by Alain Saint-Ogan in 1933. Prosper also came in a celluloid version.
CONDITION: Good
PRICE: $500-up
Book. *M. et Mme. Prosper by Alain Saint-Ogan.* Circa 1933.
CONDITION: Excellent
PRICE: $150-up
Courtesy Valerie Loiret (book), Author's collection (bear).

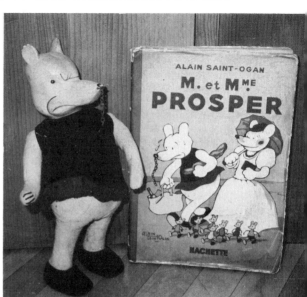

(Left) Circa 1940. 16in (41cm); pink rayon plush; short beige rayon plush in-set snout; glass eyes; f.j. (jointed with metal rods); e.s.
CONDITION: Excellent   **PRICE:** $200-up
(Front center) Circa 1940. 12in (31cm); short orange rayon plush; glass eyes; f.j. (jointed with metal rods); e.s.
CONDITION: Excellent   **PRICE:** $200-up
(Center back) Circa 1940. 16in (41cm); gold rayon plush; glass eyes; f.j. (jointed with metal rods); e.s.
CONDITION: Excellent   **PRICE:** $225-up
(Right) Circa 1940. 14in (36cm); short blue and beige rayon plush; glass eyes; f.j. (jointed with metal rods); e.s.
CONDITION: Excellent   **PRICE:** $250-up
Courtesy Ann Hood.

Polish Manufactured Bears

(Left to right) Two Bears. Circa 1970. 8in (20cm); beige and brown synthetic plush; red felt tongues; plastic eyes; f.j.; e.s. Label sewn into seam of foot reads: "R. Dakin and Co., San Francisco, CA/Product of Poland."
CONDITION: Excellent **PRICE:** $25-up each
Circa 1980. 5in (13cm); brown synthetic plush; black felt eyes; f.j.; s.s.
CONDITION: Excellent **PRICE:** $15-up

Three Bears. Circa 1985. 4in (10cm); white, beige and black sheepskin; leather lined ears, eyes and paw pads; f.j.; s.s.
CONDITION: Mint **PRICE:** $10-up (each)
Circa 1970. 7in (18cm); beige acrylic plush; black felt eyes; f.j.; s.s. Label in seam of body reads: "R. Dakin & Co., San Francisco, CA/Product of Poland."
CONDITION: Excellent **PRICE:** $15-up
Courtesy Marge Adolphson and Donnella Summers.

Unidentified Japanese Manufactured Bears

One of the most distinguishing factors in identifying Japanese teddy bears is the use of poor quality materials, such as a bright-gold, short sparse bristle mohair. On jointed bears, cardboard discs are often exposed on the outside of the arm.

A large percentage of the early jointed bears' body designs mimic the less expensive American, German and French bears, with long slender torsos, short straight arms and legs.

Circa 1930. 10in (25cm); short gold mohair; glass eyes; f.j. (jointed with wires); e.s.
CONDITION: Excellent **PRICE:** $125-up
Courtesy William H. (Bill) Boyd.

Circa 1945. 8in (20cm); creamy white celluloid; airbrushed with orange, pink and red; painted facial features; jointed arms and legs (jointed with elastic); stationary head; marked on back: "Made in Occupied Japan."
CONDITION: Mint   **PRICE: $40-up**
Courtesy William H. (Bill) Boyd.

(Left) Circa 1950. 6½in (16cm); gold rayon silk plush; beige velveteen in-set snout and paw pads; glass eyes; jointed arms; stationary head and legs; sliced-in ears; e.s. Squeaker concealed in tummy activated by pushing down on head.
CONDITION: Excellent   **PRICE: $15-up**
(Center left) Circa 1950. 6in (15cm); (Center right) 5in (13cm); pink rayon silk plush; beige velveteen in-set snout; glass eyes; jointed arms and legs; stationary heads; sliced-in ears; e.s.

(Center left)
CONDITION: Mint   **PRICE: $30-up**
(Center right)
CONDITION: Mint   **PRICE: $40-up**
(Right) Circa 1950. 7½in (19cm); cinnamon-colored artificial silk plush; beige velveteen in-set muzzle and foot pads; glass eyes; n.j.; sliced-in ears; e.s.
CONDITION: Excellent   **PRICE: $15-up**
Courtesy Marge Adolphson and Donnella Summers.

(Left to right) Walking Bear. Circa 1950. 4in (10cm); brown rayon silk plush with beige in-set snout; metal nose; glass eyes; papier-mâché body. Key wind mechanism activates walking action. CONDITION: Excellent **PRICE:** $50-up Nodding Bear. Circa 1950. 5in (13cm); black and white rayon silk plush; black and white felt eyes; plastic nose; unjointed body. Nodding head. Label on bottom of bear reads: "Made in Japan." CONDITION: Excellent **PRICE:** $25-up

Circa 1950. 5in (13cm); pink rayon silk plush; velour in-set snout; glass eyes; f.j.; e.s. CONDITION: Excellent **PRICE:** $40-up Circa 1950. 5in (13cm); black and white flannel body; celluloid head; glass eyes; unjointed arms and legs; swivel head; e.s. CONDITION: Excellent **PRICE:** $40-up *Courtesy Marge Adolphson and Donnella Summers.*

(Left) **Kamar** Polar Bear. Circa 1975. 12in (31cm); white acrylic plush; short white acrylic plush in-set snout and paw pads; black airbrushed paw design and areas of body; plastic eyes and nose; n.j.; s.s. Label sewn into seam reads: "KAMAR, Made in Japan." Hat not original to bear. CONDITION: Excellent **PRICE:** $75-up

(Right) **Kamar** *Heart Beat* Bear. Circa 1970. 11in (28cm); brown acrylic plush; short beige acrylic plush in-set snout and paw design; black airbrushed paw pads and areas of body; plastic eyes; n.j.; s.s. Label sewn into seam reads: "KAMAR." CONDITION: Excellent **PRICE:** $60-up *Courtesy Jeanne A. Miller.*

Japanese Battery-Operated Bears

The "Golden Age of the Battery-Operated Toy" took place during the 1950s and 1960s, with about 95% of all battery-operated toys sold in America and Europe originating in Japan.

Differing from other collectibles, value and collectible desirability is not based on the individual manufacturers themselves, but rather condition, the amount of separate actions and the bear's original box.

The original box increases the bear's value by approximately 10% and also the information printed on the box provides valuable information pertaining to the bear's abilities and appearance.

The more movable actions, the more valuable the bear.

S & E Co., Dentist Bear. Circa 1950. 9½in (24cm); battery operated; seven actions; (dentist) light brown plush; (patient) white plush; tin base. Dentist head moves as he drills on the little bear. When he stops he pushes his young patient's head forward to expectorate (drill lights up). Rare.
CONDITION: Mint (in box)
PRICE: $750-up
Courtesy Sandy Madden.

(Left) **A.1.** Blacksmith Bear. Circa 1950. 9in (23cm); battery-operated; black plush bear on tin base holds a horseshoe over a forge; he then moves it across to his anvil where he strikes it with his mallet. The anvil, forge and bear's eyes light up while in motion.
CONDITION: Mint
PRICE: $300-up
(Right) **T.N.** Bear the Shoemaker. Circa 1950. 9in (23cm); battery-operated; black plush bear on a tin base hammers on a boot as he shakes his head and smokes a pipe.
CONDITION: Mint
PRICE: $350-up
Courtesy Sandy Madden.

Swiss Mutzi Bears

Circa 1950. 8½in (22cm); brown mohair; glass eyes; f.j.; e.s.; metal button (red paper label is encased in metal bezel) is affixed to chest.
CONDITION: Excellent
PRICE: $300-up
Courtesy Donna Harrison-West.

Circa 1950. 8½in (22cm); honey-colored mohair; glass eyes; f.j.; e.s.; dressed as a girl in a red and white check skirt; paper C.T.; the drawing of a white bear on a black background is printed on half the tag, printed on the other half is the word "Mutzi" on a red background.
CONDITION: Mint
PRICE: $395-up
Courtesy Patricia Volpe

CHAPTER 5
MECHANICAL BEARS AND ANIMALS
Roullett et Decamps

Circa 1900. 11in (28cm); dark brown and white rabbit fur covers papier-mâché body; glass eyes; black metal nose; plaster (painted black) feet; stationary head; when wound with key, bear somersaults over trapeze bar.

CONDITION: Excellent

PRICE: $1500-up

Courtesy Patricia Volpe.

ABOVE:
(Left) Smoking Bear. Circa 1900. 20in (50.8cm); dark brown "real fur" covers papier-mâché body; carved wooden hands, feet, nose and mouth; felt tongue; glass eyes; bear permanently stands on velveteen covered base; key wind chain driven mechanism; on and off lever.
CONDITION: Excellent   **PRICE:** $3500-up
(Center) Circa 1900. 14in (36cm); dark brown "real fur" covers papier-mâché body; carved wooden feet, paws and mouth; felt tongue; glass eyes; wire muzzle; key wind chain driven mechanism; on and off lever.
CONDITION: Mint   **PRICE:** $3000-up
(Right) Jumeau Doll. Circa 1900. 24in (61cm); bisque head; glass paper weight eyes; jointed composition body.
CONDITION: Excellent   **PRICE:** $6000-up
Courtesy Harriett Early (doll). Author (bears).

Irwin

Irwin Walking Bear. Circa 1930. 12in (31cm); beige wool head and paws; cotton twill paw pads; black fabric nose; glass eyes; fabric body; wooden legs; unjointed arms; stationary head. When wound with key attached to body, bear will rock from side to side as he walks forward. Label attached to bear reads: "Darling Toddler. Wind Me Up and I Will Walk. An Irwin Product."
CONDITION: Mint   **PRICE:** $350-up
Courtesy Gregory A. Best.

Unidentified German Manufactured
Mechanical Bears and Animals

Walking Bear. Circa 1928. 14in (35cm); gold mohair; jointed arms; swivel head; stationary legs. When wound with metal key attached to bear's back, bear makes grunting sound as he walks forward.
CONDITION: Good   PRICE: $550-up
Courtesy Donna Harrison-West.

Mechanical Nodding Rabbit. Circa 1920. 27in (69cm); variegated gray artificial silk plush covers papier-mâché and wooden head, paws and body; glass eyes; original clothes. Key wind mechanism activates nodding of head and eyes to open and close.
CONDITION: Good   PRICE: $3000-up
Courtesy Brigitte Puckett.

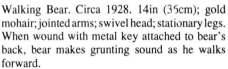

Mechanical Bear with Interchangeable Animal Heads. Circa 1930. 6in (15cm); brown rayon plush covers papier-mâché head and body; glass eyes; celluloid nose. Interchangeable dog and monkey heads. When wound with key affixed to animal's back, the head moves back and forth while the arms beat the drum and clap the cymbals. Paper label on base reads: "Made in Germany."
CONDITION: Excellent
PRICE: $450-up
Courtesy Allen and Paula Bress.

CHAPTER 6
MUSICAL BEARS AND ANIMALS

Chad Valley. Circa 1925. 20in (51cm); blue mohair; glass eyes; "wide" stitched nose; f.j.; k.s.; woven label on foot reads: "HYGIENIC TOYS MADE IN ENGLAND BY CHAD VALLEY CO. LTD." Metal button covered with clear plastic affixed to ear reads: "CHAD VALLEY HYGIENIC TOYS." Small cylinder-type music box is encased in bellows concealed in tummy. Bellows produce music when tummy is squeezed.
CONDITION: Excellent
PRICE: $1200-up
Courtesy Barbara Lauver.

Eduard Crämer. Circa 1930. 18in (46cm); pale cinnamon-colored mohair; short mohair heart-shaped face; brown cotton stitched nose; pink cotton stitched mouth (face and mouth design typical of Eduard Crämer); glass eyes; f.j.; e.s. Original orange and yellow clown hat and neck ruff. Music is produced by tilting head back and forth. Rare.
CONDITION: Good
PRICE: $2500-up

Helvetic
Musical Clown Bears. (Right) Circa 1930. 13in (33cm);
pale green long silky mohair; large glass eyes; pink stitched
nose and mouth; f.j.; e.s.; small cylinder-type music box is
encased in bellows concealed in the tummy of the bear.
Music is produced by squeezing bellows. Rare color.
Original white felt clown hat with pink pom poms.
CONDITION: Excellent   **PRICE:** $1500-up
(Left) Circa 1930. 13in (33cm); white long silky mohair;
large glass eyes; f.j.; pink stitched nose and mouth; e.s.
Music box mechanism is same as bear on left.
CONDITION: Excellent   **PRICE:** $950-up
Courtesy Patricia Volpe.

Helvetic
Musical Clown Bear. Circa 1930. 15in
(38cm); brilliant orange mohair; large glass
eyes; f.j.; e.s. A small cylinder-type music
box is encased in bellows concealed in the
tummy. Music is produced by squeezing
the bellows. Rare color. Original hat and
ruff.
CONDITION: Excellent
PRICE: $3500-up
Private collection.

Steiff. Circa 1950. 14in (36cm); golden
beige-colored mohair; glass eyes; brown
pearl cotton stitched nose and mouth; f.j.;
R.S.B.; yellow S.L.; C.T. Music box encased in body is activated by squeezing
the tummy area indicated by the original
red felt circle sewn onto bear with the
word "Music" printed on the felt.
CONDITION: Mint
PRICE: $1200-up
Courtesy Barbara Baldwin.

**See also Steiff Bears and Animals,
pages 94 and 110.**

Unidentified Manufactured Musical Bears and Animals

German. Possibly Schuco. Circa 1920. 17in (43cm); pink mohair tipped with white; glass eyes; f.j.; e.s. A small cylinder-type music box is encased in bellows. Music is activated by squeezing tummy.
CONDITION: Excellent
PRICE: $3000-up
Private collection.

MIDDLE PHOTO:
(Left) American. Circa 1910. 18in (46cm); short pale gold mohair; shoe-button eyes; f.j.; e.s. Music box is concealed in tummy; chiming music is produced when bear is moved.
CONDITION: Excellent
PRICE: $1500-up
(Center) American. Circa 1910. 10in (25cm); short pale gold mohair; glass googly-type eyes; f.j.; e.s. Music box is concealed in tummy; chiming music is produced when bear is moved.
CONDITION: Good
PRICE: $350-up
(Right) German. Circa 1920. 19in (48cm); gold mohair; glass eyes; f.j.; e.s. Small cylinder-type music box is encased in bellows concealed in tummy. Music is activated by squeezing bellows at side of torso.
CONDITION: Excellent
PRICE: $2000-up

BOTTOM PHOTO:
(Left) German. Musical Dog. Circa 1930. 10in (25cm); white and caramel-colored mohair; large glass eyes; red felt tongue; unjointed body; swivel head; e.s. Small cylinder-type music box is encased in bellows concealed in tummy. Music is activated by squeezing bellows.
CONDITION: Mint
PRICE: $500-up
(Right) German. Musical Cat. Circa 1930. 10in (25cm); blue and gray mohair; glass eyes; pink silk stitched nose and mouth; unjointed legs; swivel head; e.s. Music box action is same as dog.
CONDITION: Good
PRICE: $475-up

CHAPTER 7
ADVERTISING BEARS

National Park Souvenir Bears. Circa 1950. Sizes range from 6in (15cm) to 10in (25cm) long; short black, brown and gray synthetic plush; soft vinyl molded snout; plastic disc movable eyes and glass stick pin in eyes; n.j.; e.s. Label in seam reads: "Japan." A percentage came with tiny bells in ears. Originally came with red plastic collar and metal chain leash. Black was the most common color. CONDITION: Excellent **PRICE:** $20 - $30-up *Courtesy Marge Adolphson.*

Hamm's Bears. (Left to right) Circa 1988. 18in (46cm). Circa 1981. 14in (36cm). Circa 1960. 18in (46cm); black and white synthetic plush; plastic disc eyes; n.j.; s.s. (left and center); styrofoam beads stuffing (right). Label sewn into seam of body: "Americo Group Inc. (c)/Made in Korea."

CONDITION: Mint
PRICE: (Left) 18in (46cm) $35-up
        (Center) 14in (36cm) $25-up
        (Right) 18in (46cm) $35-up
Courtesy Marge Adolphson and Donnella Summers.

The Travel Lodge Sleepy Bears. (Back row left) Circa 1970. 18in (46cm); cinnamon-colored synthetic plush; black and white felt eyes and mouth; red pom pom nose; n.j.; s.s.; original cap and night shirt.
CONDITION: Mint
PRICE: $40-up
(Front row left) Puppet. Circa 1940. 10in (25cm); cinnamon-colored mohair body; glass eyes; black "glass" nose; beige felt mouth; n.j.; e.s.; original night shirt and cap.
CONDITION: Excellent
PRICE: $75-up
(Right) Circa 1970. 12in (31cm) (front); 18in (46cm) (back); brown synthetic plush; beige synthetic plush snout and feet; felt eyes and mouth; black pom pom nose; n.j.; s.s. 12in (31cm), styrofoam beads 18in (46cm). Orange flannel shirt and hat.
CONDITION: Mint

PRICE: 12in (31cm) $25-up
18in (46cm) $35-up

Courtesy Marge Adolphson.

Hershey's Bears. (Left back) Ideal. 1982. 12in (31cm); dark brown and white synthetic plush; soft molded vinyl face; painted features; n.j.; s.s. Label sewn into seam reads: "Ideal Toy Corp. 1982/Made in Korea."
CONDITION: Mint
PRICE: $30-up
(Left front) **Ideal.** 1982. 5½in (14cm); dark brown synthetic plush; white velour in-set snout, lining of ears, paw pads; plastic eyes; n.j.; s.s. Label sewn into seam reads: "Ideal Toy Corp. 1982/Made in Korea."
CONDITION: Mint
PRICE: $10-up
(Right) **Charles Products.** Circa 1990. 8in (20cm); brown synthetic plush; cream-colored synthetic plush in-set snout, foot pads and lining of ears; plastic eyes; plastic nose; n.j.; s.s. Label sewn into seam reads: "TM of Hersheys Food Corp./Charles Products, Licensee/Made in Korea."
CONDITION: Mint
PRICE: $20-up
Courtesy Marge Adolphson and Donnelle Summers.

CHAPTER 8
SMOKEY BEAR

Smokey the Bear came to be in a 1944 poster painted by Albert Staehle. This austere safety spokes "bear" became warmer and cuddlier when Rudy Wendelin took over the position of Smokey's official artist in 1946. He remained in that capacity for 30 years.

A live symbol of Smokey was discovered by firefighters in New Mexico in 1950. After his rescue, he lived out his life at the National Zoo in Washington D.C.

Most Smokey memorabilia is not date-marked, so it leaves that detail up to the collector to research and determine.

The Ideal Toy Company made the first Smokey Teddy Bear in 1952. It is extremely rare to find this bear with his original hat and shovel.

The Forest Service licenses a wide array of Smokey toys and other items.

Ideal Toy Company

(Left and center) 1954. 20in (51cm) [left]; 17in (43cm) [center]; brown plush; molded vinyl heads; glasene brown eyes; n.j.; s.s.; blue denim trousers. Second version of Ideal's Smokey Bear.
CONDITION: Good   **PRICE:** $95-up (left)
                                    $85-up (center)
(Right) 1953. 18in (46cm); brown plush; molded vinyl head, hands and feet; glasene eyes; painted features; n.j.; s.s.; incised on back of head "c. 1953/SMOKEY SAYS/PREVENT FOREST FIRES/IDEAL TOY COMPANY." First version

of Ideal's Smokey Bear. Smokey originally came with separate hat, blue denim trousers, blue plastic shovel and silver badge which read: "SMOKEY/RANGER/PREVENT FOREST FIRES," and a silver belt buckle which reads: "SMOKEY."
CONDITION: Excellent   **PRICE:** $150-up
(Front) Hubley Jeep. Gabriel Smokey Bear Driver. Circa 1970; plastic.
CONDITION: Mint   **PRICE:** $25-up
Courtesy Edna Brown.

Ideal Toy Company. (Left) Circa 1960. 12in (31cm); brown plush; beige plush in-set snout and paw pads; felt nose and tongue; glass eyes; n.j.; original hat and blue denim trousers; s.s. Badge reads: "Smokey Ranger Bear, Prevent Forest Fires." CONDITION: Excellent PRICE: $45-up (Center left) Circa 1953. 30in (76cm); brown plush; beige plush in-set snout; felt nose and mouth; felt eyes; n.j.; s.s.; label stitched into seam reads: "Ideal Toy Company." Dressed in light

blue denim trousers, this seated Smokey came with a compass, whistle and flashlight.
CONDITION: Excellent   PRICE: $250-up
(Center right) **Unidentified manufacturer.** Lunch Box. Circa 1970. Painted metal.
CONDITION: Excellent   PRICE: $100-up
(Right) **Unidentified manufacturer.** Smokey Bear Thermos Bottle (Metal); plastic cup.
CONDITION: Excellent   PRICE: $40-up
(Front) **Japanese** Salt and Pepper Shakers. Circa 1970. 3in (8cm). China. Marked on base: "Made in Japan/Norcrest."
CONDITION: Mint   PRICE: $15-up
Courtesy Edna Brown.

Bradley
(Left front) Pocket Watch. Circa 1970.
CONDITION: Mint
PRICE: $150-up
(Right front) Wrist Watch. Circa 1970.
CONDITION: Mint
PRICE: $100-up
(Left back) Bubble Bath Container. Circa 1970. 11in (28cm); plastic.
CONDITION: Excellent
PRICE: $10-up
(Center back) Alarm Clock. Circa 1970.
CONDITION: Mint
PRICE: $100-up
(Back right) **Art-Line Inc.** Statue. Circa 1960. 13½in (34cm); plastic.
CONDITION: Excellent
PRICE: $20-up
Courtesy Edna Brown.

Norcrest
(Left) Bank. Circa 1970. 6in (15cm); brightly painted china. Marked on base "Norcrest/Made in Japan."
CONDITION: Mint   **PRICE:** $15-up
(Center left) Bank. Circa 1970. 8in (20cm); brightly painted china. Marked on base: "Norcrest/Made in Japan."
CONDITION: Mint   **PRICE:** $20-up

(Center right) Salt and Pepper Shakers. Circa 1970. 4in (10cm); brightly painted china. Marked on base "Norcrest/Made in Japan."
CONDITION: Mint   **PRICE:** $15-up
(Right) Statue. Circa 1970. 3⅝in (10cm); brightly colored china. Marked on base: "Norcrest/Made in Japan."
CONDITION: Mint   **PRICE:** $10-up
Courtesy Edna Brown.

(Left) **Knickerbocker Toy Co.** Circa 1960. 30in (76cm); brown plush; beige plush in-set snout; felt nose and mouth; brown plastic eyes; n.j.; s.s.; blue denim trousers; monogrammed belt.
CONDITION: Good
PRICE: $125-up
(Center front) **Whitman** Smokey Bear Puzzle Tray. Circa 1969.
CONDITION: Mint
PRICE: $15-up
(Center) **R.C.A. Victor** Smokey Bear Record. Circa 1959. Sung by Eddy Arnold 78 R.P.M.
CONDITION: Excellent
PRICE: $20-up

(Center back) **Milton Bradley** Smokey Bear Game. Circa 1968.
CONDITION: Excellent   **PRICE:** $25-up
(Right) **Knickerbocker Toy Co.** Circa 1960. 15in (38cm); brown plush; cream-colored plush face; plastic eyes; felt nose and mouth; n.j.; s.s.; blue denim trousers.
CONDITION: Excellent   **PRICE:** $45-up
Courtesy Edna Brown.

R. Dakin & Co.(Left) Circa 1985. 12in (31cm); brown plush; white plush in-set snout; plastic nose and eyes; n.j.; s.s.; blue denim trousers.
CONDITION: Mint   PRICE: $20-up
(Center left) Circa 1977. 13½in (34cm); brown plush; beige plush in-set snout; felt lined open mouth; plastic eyes and nose; n.j.; s.s.; blue denim trousers; green knit sweater.
CONDITION: Mint   PRICE: $30-up
(Center) Statue. Circa 1970. 8in (20cm); plastic; cotton trousers.

CONDITION: Mint   PRICE: $25-up
(Center right) **Three Bears Inc.** Circa 1985. 15in (38cm); brown plush; cream-colored plush in-set snout; plastic eyes; fabric nose; n.j.; s.s.
CONDITION: Mint   PRICE: $25-up
(Right) Circa 1983. 10in (25cm); brown plush; cream-colored plush in-set snout; plastic eyes and nose; n.j.; s.s.
CONDITION: Mint   PRICE: $15-up
Courtesy Edna Brown.

Smokey Bear Figures.
(Back row) Circa 1968. 13in (33cm); rubber covers flexible wire armature throughout body. Embossed on back "Authorizd by U.S. Department of Agriculture. Official Smokey Bear License/In Cooperation with the State Foresters and Advertising Council Inc./.(c) 1968 Lakeside Ind./Lic. by Newfield Ltd. of England."
CONDITION: Mint   PRICE: $35-up
(Front row left to right) Circa 1967. 5½in (14cm); same information as Smokey in back row.
CONDITION: Mint   PRICE: $15-up
Circa 1970. 3¼in (9cm); hard plastic; movable arms; stationary head and legs. Embossed on back "(c) Gabriel/Auth. U.S.D.A./Made in U.K."

CONDITION: Mint   PRICE: $20-up
Circa 1970. 8in (20cm); hard plastic; movable arms; stationary head and legs; removable denim jeans; vinyl belt; gold-colored buckle; yellow plastic hat; removable shovel with words embossed "Prevent Forest Fires." Label in seam of jeans reads: "Smokey Bear/R. Dakin and Co.,/ Product of HK."
CONDITION: Mint   PRICE: $35-up
Dakin. Circa 1974. 5½in (14cm); molded soft plastic; n.j.; squeaker encased in body. Embossed on right leg: "Smokey Bear © R. Dakin and Co./ 1974/Product of HK."
CONDITION: Mint   PRICE: $20-up
Courtesy Marge Adolphson and Donnella Summers.

CHAPTER 9
ANNALEE CREATIONS

Annalee Davis Thorndike began making dolls in the kitchen of her chicken farm in 1935. At first, her dolls were predominately ski dolls but with the introduction of Annalee Dolls into major department stores in New York in the late 1950s, there was a change in creative design.

There are many traditional characteristics to be considered with Annalee Creations. Originally all the dolls had yarn hair but by the early sixties substitutions were made with synthetic plush and chicken feathers. During 1950-1954 eyes were small painted dots. This is known as the "Round Eyes" period. In 1954 Annalee's first Santa appeared and, with this the impish expression of Annalee's Creations began to emerge as dolls representing different aspects and vocations of life. Animals were first introduced in the mid-sixties.

All dolls are flexible due to their wire armature design. Most bodies are felt. In some early instances, bodies are flannel. Some Santas have velour bodies, but their faces are felt.

In 1986 Annalee® added the manufacturing date on its labels. Prior to that Annalee Mobiltee Dolls either lacked a label, or were labeled according to copyright date of the body or the head.

In 1983, the Annalee Doll Society began with 523 members. By 1992, the membership grew to more than 30,000.

Annalee is one of the largest family owned business in America. Today, at her "Factory in the Woods" in Meredith, New Hampshire, Annalee employs over 450 people. Her products continue to increase greatly in value over the years. In 1992, Annalee's 1950s "Halloween" Girl (10in [25cm]) set an auction record of $6000.

(Back left) Easter Parade Girl and Boy Bunnies. 1992. 10in (25cm); beige felt flexible bodies; painted facial features; navy and white outfits.
CONDITION: Mint
SUGGESTED ISSUE PRICE: $38.95 each.
1993 PRICE GUIDE: $75-up (each).
(Back right) Easter Parade Boy and Girl Bunnies. 1990. 10in (25cm); beige felt flexible bodies; painted facial features; green and white outfits.
CONDITION: Mint
SUGGESTED ISSUE PRICE: Boy $37.95; Girl $38.95
1993 PRICE GUIDE: $125-up (each)
(Front left) Boy and Girl Bunnies. 1978. 7in (18cm); white felt flexible head and body; painted facial features; red hair. (Red hair is highly collectible.)

CONDITION: Mint
SUGGESTED ISSUE PRICE: $5.50 each
1993 PRICE GUIDE: $175-up (each)
(Front center) Bunnies with Bushel Basket. 1977. 7in (18cm); white felt flexible bodies; painted facial features.
CONDITION: Mint
SUGGESTED ISSUE PRICE: Not available
1993 PRICE GUIDE: $175-up (set)
(Front right) Bunny with Butterfly. 1983. 7in (18cm); beige felt flexible body; painted facial features.
CONDITION: Mint
SUGGESTED ISSUE PRICE: $12.50
1993 PRICE GUIDE: $135-up
Courtesy Jeri Leslie.

(Top left) Bat. 1991. 12in (31cm); white felt body; painted facial features; black felt flexible wings; orange felt feet. Attached cord for hanging.
CONDITION: Mint
SUGGESTED ISSUE PRICE: $31.95
1993 PRICE GUIDE: $75-up
(Top right) Spider. 1991. 12in (31cm); black felt flexible body; white felt face; painted facial features; various colored flexible feet. Attached cord for hanging.
CONDITION: Mint
SUGGESTED ISSUE PRICE: $38.95
1993 PRICE GUIDE: $75-up
(Front row left to right) Merlin. 1989. 10in (25cm); beige felt flexible body; painted facial features; white beard; black outfit; holds crystal ball and wand. Edition of 2500.
CONDITION: Mint
SUGGESTED ISSUE PRICE: $69.95
1993 PRICE GUIDE: $350-up
Black Cat. 1991. 10in (25cm); black felt flexible body; painted facial features.
CONDITION: Mint
SUGGESTED ISSUE PRICE: $21.95
1993 PRICE GUIDE: Still available
Skeleton Kid. 1990. 7in (18cm); beige felt face; painted facial features; flexible body; black felt outfit; painted skeleton design on outfit; holding paper "Trick or Treat" bag. Retired December 1991.
CONDITION: Mint
SUGGESTED ISSUE PRICE: $24.45
1993 PRICE GUIDE: $150-up

Pumpkin. 1991. 13in (33cm); orange felt pumpkin; painted facial features; green felt leaves.
CONDITION: Mint
SUGGESTED ISSUE PRICE: $48.95
1993 PRICE GUIDE: Still available
Dragon Kid. 1990. 7in (18cm); beige felt flexible body; painted facial features; "red" hair; green felt outfit; holding paper "Trick or Treat" bag. Retired December 1991.
CONDITION: Mint
SUGGESTED ISSUE PRICE: $31.95
1993 PRICE GUIDE: $125-up
Witch Kid. 1990. 7in (18cm); beige felt flexible body; painted facial features; black felt outfit; holding paper "Trick or Treat" bag and broom.
CONDITION: Mint
SUGGESTED ISSUE PRICE: $27.45
1993 PRICE GUIDE: $75-up
Scarecrow. 1990. 12in (31cm); tan felt face; felt and straw flexible body; painted facial features; red felt shirt; blue denim-type overalls.
CONDITION: Mint
SUGGESTED ISSUE PRICE: $41.95
1993 PRICE GUIDE: $75-up
Duck Kid. 1989. 7in (18cm); beige felt flexible body; painted facial features; yellow, orange and black felt outfit. Retired.
CONDITION: Mint
SUGGESTED ISSUE PRICE: $25.95
1993 PRICE GUIDE: $125-up
Courtesy Jeri Leslie.

(Front) Christmas Elf. 1988. 30in (76cm); beige felt flexible body; painted facial features; red felt outfit with white trim.
CONDITION: Mint
SUGGESTED ISSUE PRICE: $54.95
1993 PRICE GUIDE: $125-up
(Back) Santa in Mechanical Rocker with Mrs. Santa and Elf (3-piece set). 1974. Santa and Mrs. Santa 29in (74cm). Elf. 22in (56cm); beige felt flexible bodies; painted facial features; red felt and cotton print outfits.
CONDITION: Mint
SUGGESTED ISSUE PRICE: $220-up
1993 PRICE GUIDE: $1750-up (3-piece set)
P.J. Kid. 1990. 12in (31cm); beige felt flexible body; painted facial features; red felt and cotton print outfit. Retired December 1991.
CONDITION: Mint
SUGGESTED ISSUE PRICE: $29.95
1993 PRICE GUIDE: $75-up
Note: Flore Bear held by Santa, not part of set. 1993 Price Guide $95-up.
Courtesy Jeri Leslie.

(Left) *Pumpkin Kid.* 1990. 18in (46cm); beige felt flexible body; painted facial features; orange felt pumpkin; green felt sweater; white felt shoes; holding paper "Trick or Treat" bag. Retired December 1991.
CONDITION: Mint
SUGGESTED ISSUE PRICE: $69.95
1993 PRICE GUIDE: $175-up
(Center) *Hobo Cat.* 1988. 15in (38cm); "white" felt face; painted facial features; purple felt coat; black felt flexible body and hat; carrying knapsack. Edition of 1600.

CONDITION: Mint
SUGGESTED ISSUE PRICE: $35.95
1993 PRICE GUIDE: $250-up
(Right) Trick or Treat Bunny Kid. 1990. 18in (46cm); beige felt flexible body; painted facial features; white felt outfit; orange felt shoes; holds paper "Trick or Treat" bag. Retired December 1991.
CONDITION: Mint
SUGGESTED ISSUE PRICE: $49.95
1993 PRICE GUIDE: $175-up
Courtesy Jeri Leslie.

(Left) *Logo Kid.* 1989. 8in (20cm); beige felt flexible body; painted facial features; yellow flannel body suit; red felt hat. Seated on rug with teddy bear and train. Dated and signed by Annalee on base. Presented as gift upon becoming a member to the Annalee Doll Society.
CONDITION: Mint
1993 PRICE GUIDE: $175-up
(Center) *Collector Doll.* (Image of Annalee). 1991. 10in (25cm); beige felt flexible body; painted facial features; pink sweater; white jacket; pink slacks; glasses perched on top of head; tape measure around neck. Surrounded by four felt 3in (8cm) kids. Mounted on a wooden base with glass dome. Signed by artist and numbered on brass plaque on base. Edition of 1914. Produced for one year only. Retired December 1991.
CONDITION: Mint
SUGGESTED ISSUE PRICE: $149.95
1993 PRICE GUIDE: $500-up
(Right) *Reading Kid.* 1991. 8in (20cm); beige felt flexible body; painted facial features; red felt pants; white cotton shirt. Seated on wooden block reading a book. Presented as a gift upon becoming a member of the Annalee Doll Society.
CONDITION: Mint
1992 PRICE GUIDE: $75-up
Courtesy Jeri Leslie.

(Left) Mouse. 1968. 12in (31cm); gray felt flexible body; painted facial features; (missing pom pom nose); purple felt hat; red and white scarf; early "wide" face design; "hand" painted face.
CONDITION: Good
SUGGESTED ISSUE PRICE: $9.95
1993 PRICE GUIDE: $350-up
(Center) Boy Bunny. 1979. 18in (46cm); beige felt flexible body; early "wide" face design; painted facial features.
CONDITION: Good
SUGGESTED ISSUE PRICE: Not available
1993 PRICE GUIDE: $95-up
(Right) Girl Bunny. 1979; beige

felt flexible body; painted facial features; white cotton outfit; beige felt hat.
CONDITION: Good   SUGGESTED RETAIL PRICE: Not available
1993 PRICE GUIDE: $95-up
American Company Wagon. Circa 1930.
CONDITION: Excellent   **PRICE:** $250-up
Courtesy Jeri Leslie.

(Right) Gingerbread Boy. 1991; beige felt flexible body; painted facial features; green felt jacket; red felt shirt; green felt scarf.
CONDITION: Mint
SUGGESTED ISSUE PRICE: $50.95
1993 PRICE GUIDE: $175-up
(Center) Flying Angel. 1990. 18in (46cm); beige felt flexible body; painted facial features; white felt flexible wings; holding metal trumpet. Retired December 1991.
CONDITION: Mint
SUGGESTED ISSUE PRICE: $51.95
1993 PRICE GUIDE: $225-up
(Left) Toy Soldier. 1990. 18in (46cm); beige flexible felt body; painted facial features; red felt jacket; black felt trousers; white felt gloves; black felt hat.
CONDITION: Mint
SUGGESTED ISSUE PRICE: $54.95
1993 PRICE GUIDE: $175-up
(Front left) Christmas Panda with Toy Bag. 1986. 10in (25cm); black and white felt flexible body; painted facial features; red felt hat; green scarf; red mittens; green felt toy bag. Edition of 4397.
CONDITION: Mint
SUGGESTED ISSUE PRICE: $18.95
1993 PRICE GUIDE: $250-up
(Front right) Santa with Train Set. 1990. 18in (46cm); beige felt flexible bodies; painted facial features; red felt trousers; green felt waistcoat; green and white print cotton shirt; black felt shoes. Electric train.
CONDITION: Mint
SUGGESTED ISSUE PRICE: $119.95
1993 PRICE GUIDE: $450-up
Courtesy Jeri Leslie.

Animal Series. Limited Edition of 3000 of each animal. All animals have signed (by artist) and numbered brass plaques. All are retired pieces.
(Left to right) Penguin with Baby. 1985. 10in (25cm); black and white felt; flexible bodies; painted facial features; gold felt beaks.
CONDITION: Mint
SUGGESTED ISSUE PRICE: $37.50
1993 PRICE GUIDE: $500-up
Owl. 1988. 5½in (14cm); beige and brown felt; flexible body; painted facial features; gold felt beak. Carries book.
CONDITION: Mint
SUGGESTED ISSUE PRICE: $37.50
1993 PRICE GUIDE: $600-up
Kangaroo with Baby. 1987. 10in (25cm); tan felt; flexible bodies; painted facial features; red and white scarf.
CONDITION: Mint
SUGGESTED ISSUE PRICE: $37.50
1993 PRICE GUIDE: $500-up
Unicorn. 1986. 10in (25cm); white felt; flexible body; painted facial features.
CONDITION: Mint
SUGGESTED ISSUE PRICE: $37.50
1993 PRICE GUIDE: $550-up
Thorndike Chicken. 1990. 5in (13cm); reddish-brown felt body; yellow felt legs, feet and beak; flexible body; painted facial features; carrying egg and staff.
CONDITION: Mint
SUGGESTED ISSUE PRICE: $37.50
1993 PRICE GUIDE: $550-up
Polar Bear Cub. 1989. 5½in (14cm); white felt; flexible body; painted facial features; holding fishing pole; fish laying on base.
CONDITION: Mint
SUGGESTED ISSUE PRICE: $37.50
1993 PRICE GUIDE: $500-up
Courtesy Jeri Leslie.

CHAPTER 10
RAGGEDY ANN & ANDY DOLLS

Johnny Gruelle created Raggedy Ann and Andy as a living memory to his own little girl who died young. One of her favorite toys was a rag doll which was the prototype of Raggedy Ann.

Based on Gruelle's story, the first Ann had dark brown hair and her brother, auburn. Initially Ann and Andy did not look alike, but by the mid 1930s they resembled each other. By the next decade, their hair turned carrot color, but the bright red hair we know today did not evolve until the 1980s.

Early commercial Raggedy Ann and Andy Dolls had stiff cardboard hearts which could be felt through the stuffing. Today this tradition is carried out with a heart imprinted or embroidered on the fabric body.

The early examples of this doll bear a copyright date of September 7, 1915 and were manufactured by P.F. Volland Company.

For a brief year (1934-35) the Exposition Toy and Doll Company made the brother and sister rag dolls. Mollye's Doll Outfitters proved to be fierce competition and made more than $1 million before the Gruelle family won a lawsuit curtailing production of Raggedy Ann and Andy by this greedy company.

In 1938, the Gruelles linked up with Georgene Novelties which then made Raggedy dolls for a quarter of a century.

In 1962, the Knickerbocker Toy Company took over the manufacturing and this is when the hair went from orange to red. The Applause Company now licenses Raggedy Ann and Andy dolls through Hasbro. Worth Gruelle, John B. Gruelle's son, presently owns the Raggedy license.

P.F. Volland Raggedy Ann and Andy Dolls. Circa 1920. 16in (41cm) to 18in (46cm); cloth bodies; painted facial features; black button eyes; n.j.; s.s
CONDITION: Excellent
PRICE:
Raggedy Ann 16in (41cm)
$1500-up (each)
Raggedy Andy 18in (46cm)
$1200-up (each)
Courtesy Candy Brainard.

(Front) **Mollye Goldman's** Raggedy Ann and Andy dolls. Circa 1935. 18in (46cm); cloth bodies; painted facial features; nose outlined in black; reddish-orange hair; n.j.; s.s. Ann has blue floral dress; blue shoes and multicolored striped legs (an integral part of body). Andy has blue pants; multicolored checkered shirt; blue shoes and multicolored striped socks (an integral part of body). Printed on chest: "Raggedy Ann and Andy Dolls Manufactured by Mollye's Doll Outfitters." Within the year after the Volland Company ceased production of the doll, Mollye Goldman began producing her version. Produced under the name Mollye's Doll Outfitters, the company only produced Raggedys from 1935 to 1938.
CONDITION: Fair   **PRICE:** $450-up (each)
(Back left) **P.F. Volland** Raggedy Ann. Circa 1920. 16in (41cm); cloth body; shoe-button eyes; painted facial features; brown yarn hair; n.j.; s.s.; "cardboard heart" concealed in body. Patent date stamped on torso reads: "September 7, 1915." Original clothes. Rare.
CONDITION: Mint   **PRICE:** $1700-up

(Back right) **P.F. Volland** Raggedy Andy. Circa 1920. 17½in (45cm); cloth body; shoe-button eyes; painted facial features; auburn yarn hair; n.j.; s.s. Early Andys had a separate shirt and pants and slightly longer legs to accommodate the pants. A percentage had oversized hands and very large thumbs.
CONDITION: Excellent   **PRICE:** $1300-up

OPPOSITE PAGE:
Mollye Internationals. Raggedy Ann Doll. Circa 1930. 22in (56cm); painted facial features; nose outlined in black; reddish-orange hair; n.j.; s.s.; floral cotton dress; white pinafore; blue shoes and multicolored striped legs (an integral part of body). Printed on front of torso: "Raggedy Ann and Andy/Manufactured by Mollye Doll Outfitters." This was the first known company to imprint a solid red heart on the chest of the doll. Rare, especially in this condition.
CONDITION: Mint   **PRICE:** $1000-up
Courtesy Nancy Torode.

(Left) **Knickerbocker Toy Company.** *Beloved Belindy.* Doll. Circa 1965. 16in (41cm); cloth body; painted face (no outline to nose); large flat black button eyes; n.j.; s.s.; one-piece red and yellow dress with white polka dots; white pantaloons; red bandanna; red shoes and red and white striped socks (an integral part of body). Label sewn into seam of dress: "Joy of A Toy Knickerbocker/Knickerbocker Toy Company Inc." Reverse of tag: "Beloved Belinda/Bobbs-Merrell Co., Inc. 1963."
CONDITION: Excellent   **PRICE:** $350-up
(Right) **Georgene Novelties Co. Inc.** *Beloved Belindy.* Doll. Circa 1940. 17in (43cm); cloth body; painted face; nose outlined in black; large flat black button eyes; n.j.; s.s.; red, white and yellow polka dotted dress; red bandanna; red shoes and red and white striped socks (an integral part of body). Manufacturer's stamp on back of head.
CONDITION: Excellent   **PRICE:** $1000-up

P.F. Volland Raggedy Ann doll. Circa 1920. 16in (41cm); cloth body; shoe-button eyes; painted facial features; dark brown hair; n.j.; s.s.; floral cotton dress; white pinafore; white pantaloons; black shoes; red and white striped legs (an integral part of body). Note: "One" lower line under eye. Known as the "teardrop" face. Very rare.
CONDITION: Mint   **PRICE:** $1700-up
Courtesy Nancy Torode.

(Left) **Georgene Novelties Co. Inc.** Raggedy Andy Doll. Circa 1950. 16in (41cm); cloth body; shoe-button eyes; painted facial features; n.j.; s.s. CONDITION: Excellent **PRICE:** $100-up (Right) **Georgene Novelties Co. Inc.** Raggedy Ann. Circa 1950. Raggedy Ann doll. 20in (51cm); cloth body; shoe-button eyes; painted facial features; n.j.; s.s. CONDITION: Excellent **PRICE:** $175-up

(Left to right) **Knickerbocker Toy Company** Raggedy Ann and Andy Dolls. Circa 1965. 16in (41cm); cloth bodies; painted facial features; flat black button eyes; red hair; n.j.; s.s. Ann is wearing floral dress; white pinafore; white pantaloons; black shoes and red and white striped legs (an integral part of body). Andy is wearing blue pants; red and white checked shirt (one-piece outfit); blue and white hat; black shoes and red and white striped legs (an integral part of body).
CONDITION: Excellent **PRICE:** $35-up (each)
Knickerbocker Toy Company. Raggedy Andy. Original box. Circa 1960. 14in (36cm); cloth body; painted face; flat black button eyes; red hair; n.j.; s.s.
CONDITION: Excellent   **PRICE:** $100-up

American Toy and Novelty Mfg. Co. Raggedy Andy. Circa 1950. 15in (38cm); cloth body; painted facial features (nose outlined in painted black stitches); reddish-orange hair; n.j.; s.s.; blue cotton pants; red and blue checked shirt; blue and white hat; blue shoes and multicolored striped legs (an integral part of body).
CONDITION: Fair   **PRICE:** $150-up
Georgene Novelties Inc. Raggedy Andy Doll. Circa 1940. 19in (48cm); cloth body; painted facial features (nose outlined in black); large black button eyes; red hair; n.j.; s.s.; blue cotton pants; red checked shirt; blue and white striped (wide spaced stripes) legs (an integral part of body). Georgene Novelty Company produced Raggedy Ann and Andy dolls from 1938 to 1962.
CONDITION: Good   **PRICE:** $375-up

CHAPTER 11
GOLLIWOGS

Interest in Golliwogs is increasing. First popular in England at the turn-of-the-century, this doll, with wild fuzzy black hair, bright red smile and white outlined eyes was based on a series of books illustrated by Florence K. Upton

Dean's Rag Book Company and Merrythought Ltd. still produce these intriguing toys today.

(Left) **Steiff**. Circa 1913. 18in (46cm); black felt face with formed nose; shoe-button eyes backed with white and red felt circles; red felt applied mouth; black mohair hair; black felt hands; f.j.; e.s.; bright non-removable blue felt jacket; white shirt and vest; red bow tie; loose fitting red trousers; FF button. Steiff produced their first Golliwog in 1908 and he remained in production until 1916 or 1917. He was available in a range of sizes from 11in (28cm) to 39in (98cm). Very rare.
CONDITION: Excellent
PRICE: $10,500-up

(Center and right) **Kathy Thomas**. 1990 (Center) 5in (13cm); (Right) 8in (20cm); black ultrasuede faces with formed noses; small black glass eyes backed with red and white ultrasuede circles; f.j.; s.s.; red, blue and white ultrasuede clothes (an integral part of body); black leather boots. Limited edition 10 of each size.
CONDITION: Mint
PRICE: Center $325-up
        Right $350-up
Courtesy Kathy Thomas.

(Left) **Merrythought.** Circa 1960. 12in (31cm); black felt face and hands; white button-type eyes with black painted pupils; red felt mouth; black wool hair; n.j.; k.s.; brightly colored clothes (an integral part of body).
CONDITION: Excellent   **PRICE:** $175-up
(Center) Homemade. Circa 1915. Black cotton sateen head and body; eyes are white cardboard circles with black embroidered pupils; embroidered mouth; black seal fur hair; n.j.; e.s.; peach rayon dress.

CONDITION: Good   **PRICE:** $200-up
(Right) **Unidentified British manufacturer.** Circa 1915. 22in (56cm); black cotton sateen face and hands; black shoe-button eyes over white shirt buttons; red felt mouth; black twisted yarn hair; unjointed arms and legs; swivel head; k.s.; red shoes and gray and white suit (an integral part of body); green jacket; red bow tie.
CONDITION: Excellent   **PRICE:** $375-up
Courtesy Kathy Thomas.

Unidentified Manufactured Golliwogs

(Left) Homemade Doll. Circa 1920. 11in (28cm); black cotton sateen head and body; mother of pearl button eyes; embroidered facial features; Persian lamb hair; n.j.; k.s.; purple velvet coat; silk pants and shoes.
CONDITION: Good
PRICE: $175-up
(Right) **Unidentified British manufacturer.** Circa 1925. 11in (28cm); black cotton sateen face, hands and feet; shoe-button eyes backed with white shirt buttons; red felt mouth; black cotton plush hair; n.j.; k.s.; clothes (an integral part of body.) Note unusual shape of leg denotes 1920s period.
CONDITION: Excellent
PRICE: $165-up
Courtesy Kathy Thomas.

British. Circa 1926. 13in (33cm); black velveteen; white milk glass eyes with painted black pupils; embroidered mouth and nose; black mohair hair; n.j.; k.s.; red and blue velvet suit (an integral part of body).
CONDITION: Excellent   **PRICE: $225-up**
Courtesy Kathy Thomas.

BELOW:
(Left) British. Circa 1950. 30in (76cm); black rayon face; plastic disc eyes; red rayon applied mouth; black mohair hair; n.j.; s.s.; red pants; yellow and white checked shirt; black and white felt jacket, gloves and shoes (clothes an integral part of body). Elastic bands affixed to shoes to enable Golliwog to be attached to your shoes to make him a dancer.
CONDITION: Excellent   **PRICE: $225-up**
(Center) British. Circa 1980. 36in (91cm); black rayon face, hands and feet; printed facial features; black plush hair; n.j.; e.s.; brightly colored plush clothes (an integral part of body).
CONDITION: Excellent   **PRICE: $150-up**
(Right) **Chad Valley**. Circa 1960. 36in (91cm); short black plush face; plastic disc eyes backed with white felt; red felt mouth; brightly colored plush outfit (an integral part of body); n.j.; s.s.
CONDITION: Excellent   **PRICE: $250-up**
Courtesy Kathy Thomas.

British. Circa 1950. Sizes (left to right) 12in (31cm); 9in (23cm); 12in (31cm); 8in (20cm). All Golliwogs have black cotton faces with printed facial features (with the exception of Golliwog on right, its face is rexine [a type of oilcloth] with painted features); black plush hair; n.j.; k.s.; clothes (an integral part of body.)
CONDITION: Excellent   **PRICE:** (Left to right): $85-up; $75-up; $90-up; $95-up
Courtesy Kathy Thomas.

Barbara Conley - Roley Bear Company.
(Back) 1984. 24in (61cm); honey-colored mohair; antique glass eyes; f.j.; e.s. Featured on
postcards, calendars, books and puzzles.
CONDITION: Mint   **PRICE:** $1000-up

(Front) 1989. 13in (33cm); off-white mohair;
antique shoe-button eyes; f.j.; e.s.
CONDITION: Mint   **PRICE:** $250-up
Courtesy Barbara Conley.

CHAPTER 12
ARTIST BEARS

An important impact on the popularity and growth of the teddy bear market are the talented efforts of a new breed of teddy bear artists. Early antique bears are increasingly difficult to find as well as expensive. With a deep affection for these little furry characters more and more collectors choose to seek out the excellent workmanship, individuality and quality of today's handmade teddy bears.

Original concept, fine workmanship, flair and style set these bearmakers apart from the crowd. As the ongoing demand for old bears continues to drive prices higher and higher, the demand for bears made by independent bear artists is growing even faster with prices climbing.

Corla Cubillas - The Dancing Needle. *The Sandman's Visit.* 1991. *Binkie* (laying in bed). 14in (36cm); honey-colored mohair; glass eyes; f.j.; posable armature encased in body; pellet stuffing. Wearing vintage nightgown. *Sandman.* 20in (51cm); honey-colored mohair; glass eyes; f.j.; s.s. Wearing tan-colored wool robe and night cap (night cap decorated with small bear's head). One-of-a-kind. Created for the 1991 Walt Disney® World Teddy Bear Auction.
CONDITION: Mint
PRICE: $1200-up
Courtesy Corla Cubillas.

Martha De Raimo - Bear-y Patch. *Forest Guardian and Apprentice.* 1992. (Left) 6in (15cm); tan-colored distressed mohair; glass eyes; f.j.; s.s.
(Right) 17in (43cm); gold distressed mohair; shoe-button eyes; f.j.; s.s. Bears are dressed in antique lace and beadwork. The tiny fireflies surrounding the small bear and the wand carried by the larger bear light up by means of electricity. One-of-a-kind. Created for the 1992 Walt Disney® World Teddy Bear Auction.
CONDITION: Mint
PRICE: $2000-up
Courtesy Martha De Raimo.

Flore Emory - Flore Bears. *Thanksgiving Celebration.* 1989. (Front row, left to right) Children. 9in (23cm); 11in (28cm). (Back row, left to right) Pilgrim Man. 20in (51cm); Indian Chief. 24in (61cm); Indian Squaw. 16in (41cm); Pilgrim Woman. 20in (51cm). Various tan-colored shades of acrylic plush; glass eyes; f.j.; s.s. Label sewn into seam reads: "Flore."
CONDITION: Mint
PRICE:
    Child (9in [23cm]) $85-up
    Child (11in [28cm]) $90-up
    Pilgrim (man) (20in [51cm]) $150-up
    Indian Chief (24in [61cm]) $250-up
    Indian Squaw (16in [41cm]) $50-up
    Pilgrim (woman) (20in [51cm]) $150-up
Courtesy Flore Emory.

Sue and Randall Foskey - Nostalgic Bears. *Cinderbearra.* 1990. 27½in (70cm); beige-colored mohair; black glass eyes; f.j.; s.s. Dressed in full-length French blue cotton dress with white print apron. With her is a bird of canary mohair (4½in [11cm]) and a f.j. mouse (4¾in [12cm]) of caramel and white mohair. One-of-a-kind. Created for the 1990 Walt Disney® World Teddy Bear Auction.
CONDITION: Mint   **PRICE:** $1000-up
Courtesy Sue and Randall Foskey.

Diane Gard - A Bear With A Heart. *Young Jacques and his Cat, Calypso.* 1991. Bear - 30in (76cm); gold distressed mohair; glass eyes; jointed arms and legs; s.s. Cat - 12in (31cm) tall; black and white mohair; glass eyes; jointed arms and legs; s.s. Created for the 1991 Walt Disney World®Teddy Bear Auction.
CONDITION: Mint
PRICE: $1500-up
Courtesy George B. Black, Jr.

Elaine Fujita-Gamble - Fujita-Gamble Teddies. (Left and right) Little Girl Bears. 1988. 2½in (6cm); beige upholstery fabric; black bead eyes; f.j.; s.s.; silk dresses trimmed with antique ribbons, lace and beads. CONDITION: Mint **PRICE:** $125-up (each) (Center) Baby Bear. 1988. 1¾in (5cm); beige upholstery fabric; black bead eyes; f.j.; s.s. CONDITION: Mint **PRICE:** $75-up *Courtesy Elaine Fujita-Gamble.*

BELOW:
Ann Inman - Annemade Bears.
Bear. 1991. 26in (66cm); beige al-
paca; black glass eyes; flexible ar-
mature encased throughout body;
s.s.
CONDITION: Mint
PRICE: $600-up
Trike. Circa 1930. 20in (51cm).
CONDITION: Excellent
PRICE: $400-up
Mannequin. 1990. 37in (94cm).
CONDITION: Excellent
PRICE: $250-up
Courtesy Alan and Dorothy Scholz.

ABOVE:
Linda Henry - Bearloom Bears.
Romeo and Juliet. 1992. 20in
(51cm); hand-dyed mohair; por-
celain faces (custom mixed to
match the mohair hand-carved to
simulate fur); f.j.; s.s. Period cos-
tumes made of velvet. Limited
edition of 5 sets.
CONDITION: Mint
PRICE: $1500-up (pair)
Courtesy Linda Henry.

OPPOSITE PAGE:
**Donna Hodges - Bearons of La
Jolla.** *Father Christmas of the
Woodland Bears.* 1991. 14in
(36cm); 16in (41cm); 18in
(46cm); 20in (51cm); and 24in
(61cm). Various colors of variegated distressed mohair; black
glass eyes; f.j.; fiber stuffing; 14in
(36cm) bear plastic pellet stuffing. *Father Christmas.* Created
by Shelie Robertson. 5ft (152cm).
Set limited edition of 10.
CONDITION: Mint
PRICE: $3900-up (set)
Courtesy Donna Hodges.

Mary Holstad - Mary
Holstad and Friends. *And*
There She Is. Papa. 18in
(46cm); *Mama.* 17in (43cm);
Baby. 11½in (29cm); Ger-
man-tipped dark brown mo-
hair; glass eyes; f.j.; s.s.
Goldilocks. 13in (33cm); head
and hands hand-sculpted in
cernit (a petrol l eum-based
clay); body is single knot fabric with coire in arms; hand
painted features. One-of-a-
kind. Created for the 1992 First
Annual Disneyland Teddy
Bear Classic Auction.
CONDITION: Mint
PRICE: $2000-up
Courtesy Mary Holstad.

Cindy Martin - Yesterbears.
1990. Sizes range from 4in
(10cm) to 20in (51cm); white
mohair; glass eyes; f.j.; s.s.
CONDITION: Mint
PRICE: $325 to $750-up
Courtesy Ho Phi Le. Photo-
graph by Ho Phi Le.

Joanne Mitchell - Family Tree Bears. *Paws for Peace.* 1990. 18in (46cm); brown plush; f.j. (flexible armature encased in arms and legs); needlesculptured nose of kid; lead crystal eyes (exclusive traits of Family Tree Bears); s.s. The fabric of the globe is patterned and needle punched to create the dimensions of continents. The tree stump is designed and created with simulated bark. Mounted on a finished cedar platform with inscribed brass plate. Limited edition of 50. Originally created for the 1990 Walt Disney World® Teddy Bear Convention. Paws for Peace was also awarded winner of the First Annual TOBY® Awards, sponsored and produced by *Teddy Bear and friends*® magazine and Hobby House Press, Inc., in 1990 (category "Artist Bear/ Large").
CONDITION: Mint
PRICE: $2000-up

Joanne Mitchell - Family Tree Bears. *Marc Antony and Cleopatra VII.* 1992. (Left) *Marc Antony.* 29in (74cm); beige mohair; black glass eyes; f.j. (flexible armature throughout arms); s.s.; maroon suede civrass with overlapping scales decorated with gold medallions; white linentype tunic; maroon velvet cloak; leather sandals.
(Right) *Cleopatra.* 28in (71cm); white mohair; glass eyes; f.j. (flexible armature throughout arms); s.s.; authentically outfitted in white silk and blue satin dress adorned with jewels; beaded headdress crowned with the symbol of a vulture; handmade gold sandals.
CONDITION: Mint
PRICE: $5000-up (pair)
Courtesy Ringstads Collection.

Kathy Mullin - Mulbeary's.
(Left) Rabbit. 1989. 26in (66cm);
brown tipped in white acrylic plush;
glass eyes; pink stitched nose; f.j.;
s.s.; brown jacket; cream-colored
waistcoat; brown checked bow tie
and top hat. One-of-a-kind.
CONDITION: Mint
PRICE: $475-up
(Right) Rabbit. 1989. 26in (66cm);
white acrylic plush; glass eyes; pink
stitched nose outlined in black; f.j.;
s.s.; maroon and blue silk jacket. One-
of-a-kind. These two rabbit designs
are based on the White Rabbit and
Mad Hatter characters in the story
Alice in Wonderland.
CONDITION: Mint
PRICE: $475-up
Courtesy Susan Wiley.

Gisele Nash - Cinnamon Bears and Friends.
(Left) *Uncle Salty* Bear. 1992 17in (43cm);
brown acrylic plush; hand-sculpted cinnamon
composition (a composite of cinnamon and other
ingredients) face; hand-painted face; f.j.; s.s.;
(Right) Cecil Seagull. 1992 4½in (12cm); white
felt; hand-sculpted Sculpy® face; hand-painted
face; glass eyes; n.j.; s.s.
CONDITION: Mint
PRICE: $160-up
(Front) *Uncle Salty and Cecil* Figurine. 1992.
5½in (14cm); hand-sculpted in Sculpy®; hand
painted.
CONDITION: Mint
PRICE: $50-up
Courtesy Gisele Nash.

ABOVE:
Robert Raikes - Original Woody Bears.
(Left) Chelsea-face Woody Bear. 1986.
18in (46cm); black acrylic fur; hand-carved
face and paw pads; in-set plastic eyes; f.j.;
s.s.; hand-carved on foot "4/25 Raikes
1986." Dressed in pink and white "party
dress" with matching bow (at ear).
CONDITION: Mint   **PRICE:** $2000-up
(Center left) Pouty-face Ballerina. Woody
Bear. 1985. 18in (46cm); cream-colored
acrylic fur; s.s.; hand-carved wooden face
and paw pads; in-set plastic eyes; f.j.; s.s.;
hand-carved on foot "Raikes '85 MS032."
Dressed in pink tulle tutu and pink rose (at
ear).
CONDITION: Mint   **PRICE:** $1900-up
(Center right) Sailor. Woody Bear. 1985.
18in (46cm); brown acrylic fur; s.s.; hand-
carved wooden face and paw pads; hand
painted freckles on snout; in-set plastic
eyes; f.j.; s.s.; hand-carved on foot "Raikes
'85 MS028." Dressed in white and blue
sailor suit.
CONDITION: Mint   **PRICE:** $1900-up
(Right) Pouty-face Woody Bear. 1986.
18in (46cm); snowy white acrylic fur; hand-
carved face and paw pads; in-set plastic
eyes; f.j.; s.s.; hand-carved on foot "Robert
Raikes 2/25 1986." Dressed in knitted dark
blue and white scarf and hat, with the
words "Woody Bear" knitted into scarf.
CONDITION: Mint   **PRICE:** $1900-up
Courtesy Janice and Peter Spitzer.

Laurie Sasaki - Thimble-Bearries. Nutcracker Bear.
1990. 3in (8cm); tan synthetic flocked velvet; glass bead
eyes; f.j.; s.s.; brightly colored outfit and black leather
boots an integral part of body. One-of-a-kind.
CONDITION: Mint   **PRICE:** $400-up

ABOVE:
**Maria Schmidt - The Charlestown(
Bear.** Clown Bears. 1990. 23in (58cm)
curly pink mohair bodies; white mohair heads and paws; glass eyes; em-
bellished around eyes with ribbon
embroidery technique; purple sequin'
around wrists and ankles; f.j.; s.s.
CONDITION: Mint
PRICE: $700-up
Courtesy Maria Schmidt.

Steve Schutt - Bear-"s"-ence. Ham-
Bear-Grrrr. 1991. 12in (31cm); dark
brown antique buffalo pile; antique
shoe-button eyes; f.j.; s.s. Bun is silk
over styrofoam painted with acrylic
paint; silk lettuce; felt cheese, mustard
and catsup; dried oranges are painted
with acrylic paint for tomatoes and
pickles. One-of-a-kind.
CONDITION: Mint
PRICE: $1000-up
Courtesy Steve Schutt.

A representation of the highly sought-after **Bearly There Company** bears created by Linda Spiegel-Lohre. This outstanding group depicts some of the distinctive and appealing characteristics of Linda's designs. Ranging in size and approximate price from 5in (13cm) - $40.00 (plush); 7in (18cm) - $68.00 (mohair) to 18in (46cm) - $68.00 (plush), $195.00 (mohair).
Courtesy Linda Spiegel-Lohre.

My little grand-children Jenny Mullins (left) and Frances Tipton (right) especially love petting these two bears when they visit Nana's house. These magnificent examples of a mother bear and her cub were created by Joan Woessner and her son Michael J. Woessner.
(Left) *Moma Black Bear.* 1992. 40in (101cm) long by 21in (53cm) tall; hand-sculpted black alpaca; taxidermist bear eyes; fiberglass form; polyfill stuffing; n.j.; hand-sculpted nose and claws. Limited edition of 50
CONDITION: Mint   **PRICE:** $2200-up
(Right) *Baby Black Bear.* 1992. 22in (56cm) tall; hand-sculpted black alpaca; taxidermist bear eyes; fiberglass form; polyfill stuffing; n.j.; hand-sculpted nose and claws. Limited edition of 100.
CONDITION: Mint   **PRICE:** $1000-up

Joan Woessner - Bear Elegance. *Ride into Fantasyland.* 1991. (Left to right) Goose. 24in (61cm) long by 16in (41cm) tall; white mohair; leather feet and beak; posable neck and wings; glass eyes; s.s. Jester. 10in (25cm); brown and mauve mohair; glass eyes; f.j.; mauve jester hat. Jester. 26in (66cm); brown and mauve mohair; glass eyes; s.s. Jester outfit mauve silk with gold trims. Hat silk brocade. Pruitts Place Enchanted Swan. 25in (64cm) by 16in (41cm). Ride into Fantasyland was the winning entry of the 1991 TOBY® Award in two categories - Large Artist Bear/Dressed and Artist's Character Teddy Award. CONDITION: Mint   PRICE: $2500-up *Courtesy Rob and Inge Kutters.*

R. John Wright Dolls Inc. (Left) *Winnie-the-Pooh.* 1988. 14in (36cm); honey-gold English plush; glass eyes; f.j.; s.s.; brass button attached to body inscribed: "RJW;" small stuffed bee attached to bear's ear; custom-made honey pot. Licensed by permission of The Walt Disney® Company. Limited edition of 5000.
CONDITION: Mint   PRICE: $395-up (Center) *Christopher Robin.* 1985. 18in (46cm); 100% wool felt; painted facial features; f.j.; s.s.; blue cotton jacket; brown cotton shorts; white cotton hat; brown leather shoes; paper tag attached to jacket reads "R. John Wright Dolls Inc/Christopher Robin & Winnie the Pooh/No 0197/1000 (c) Walt Disney® Productions."
(Right) *Winnie-the-Pooh.* 1985. 8in (20cm); caramel-colored custom-made 100% wool "coating;" black glass eyes; f.j.; s.s.; maroon knit jacket; tag attached to jacket reads: "R John Wright Dolls Inc/Winnie the Pooh. No 0197/2500. (c) Walt Disney® Productions."
CONDITION: Mint   PRICE: $1800-up (*Christopher Robin* and *Winnie-the-Pooh* sold originally as a set)

R. John Wright Creations

NAME OF EDITION	SIZE	NUMBER IN EDITION	INTRODUCED	1993 PRICE
Christopher Robin & Winnie-the-Pooh		1000	1985-6	$1800-up
Winnie-the-Pooh	8in (20cm)	2500	1985-6	$600-up
Piglet	5½in (13cm)	1000	1985-6	$395-up
Eeyore		1000	1986-7	$395-up
Kanga & Roo		1000	1986-7	$295-up
Tigger		1000	1986-7	$295-up
Christopher Robin - Series (with raincoat and umbrella)		500	1986-7	$1500-up
Winnie-the-Pooh ("life-size")	20in (51cm)	2500	1986-7	$695-up
Piglet ("life-size")	10½ (27cm)	1000	1986-7	$295-up
Winnie-the-Pooh with honey pot	14in (36cm)	5000	1988-9	$395-up
Piglet with Violets	7½in (18cm)	2500	1988-9	$200-up
Winnie-the-Pooh & his favorite chair	10in (25cm) height of Pooh	500	1988-9	$850-up

OTHER DISTINGUISHED REFERENCE BOOKS BY THE AUTHOR

Linda Mullins is regarded as the premier Teddy Bear Show promoter in America. She is a leading authority in teddy bear collecting.

TEDDY BEARS PAST & PRESENT, VOLUME I

Regarded as THE COLLECTOR'S IDENTIFICATION GUIDE, this volume contains a wealth of critical background information on the history of leading bear manufacturers and over 600 photographs, 80 in color, of the bears they produced. *Teddy Bears Past & Present* makes it easy to determine the price of your favorite bears because of its visual and chronological order. Best presentation about the distinguishing characteristics of bears, labels and tags. 304 pages. 8½" x 11". HB. Item #3120. $29.95

TEDDY BEARS PAST & PRESENT, VOLUME II

As the companion to Volume I, *Teddy Bears Past & Present, II* provides more in depth research into the gems of the history of the teddy bear. This research includes such diverse topics as today's bruin collecting and manufacturing in Germany, America, Britain, Australia, Japan and France as well as biographies of elite teddy bear artists and a wealth of photographs of their bears. Over 500 photos, 153 in stunning full-color. 304 pages. 8½" x 11". HB. Item #H4330. $25.00

TEDDY BEAR MEN

Retrace the beginnings of the teddy bear and see and learn about the collectibles and cartoons of President Theodore Roosevelt and Clifford Berryman as they relate to the teddy bear. Discover how President Roosevelt saved a little bruin's life and started a teddy bear craze and how cartoonist Clifford Berryman helped the cuddly creature achieve his present day status of THE TEDDY BEAR. 160 pages. 51 color photos. 8½" x 11". PB. Item #3590. $6.95

THE RAIKES BEAR & DOLL STORY

At last, Robert Raikes fans have something to cheer about! An exquisite photograph album and very readable story of how Raikes' phenomenal bears came to be and their evolution into one of the hottest bear collectibles ever. Includes fascinating photos of the early carvings through the bears and dolls produced in 1990 as well as some exquisite one-of-a-kind pieces. 112 pages. 234 total photographs, 146 in color! 8½" x 11". HB. Item #H4158. $19.95

4TH TEDDY BEARS & FRIENDS®
PRICE GUIDE

Latest values on bears, rabbits, cats and dogs as well as a wealth of other animals are featured! This book shows and values what is being collected today! Such important collectibles as Muffy, antique, collectible, manufacturer and artist are featured as well as a large section devoted to such popular companies as Steiff, North American Bear, Gund and limited editions from Steiff Museum Collection. Charts as well as 358 stunning photographs capturing the character of bears and their friends. 176 pages. 118 color photos. 6" x 9". PB. Item #H4438. $12.95

Back Cover
(Top photo) Jenny Mullins (author's six-year-old granddaughter) has fun posing in the 1930 Packard child's pedal car. All original (partially repainted). Rare.
CONDITION: Excellent   **PRICE:** $8500-up
(Bottom photo) Steiff Animated Display. Circa 1948. 21 ft (640cm) by 7 ft (213cm).
Rare. *(See page 121 for more information.)*
Condition: Good   **PRICE:** $20,000-up

ABOUT THE AUTHOR

Linda Mullins, born and raised in England, emigrated to America in 1969. Some of her first memories are of the London air raids of World War II. She recalls her mother rushing her and her beloved teddy bear to the safety of the bomb shelter. Her lifelong love affair with the Teddy Bear has never ended. When her husband, Wally, gave her an antique teddy bear as a gift, her collection began.

Linda soon became aware of the pleasures of collecting. That suspense of discovering hidden treasure and the satisfaction of preserving the wonders of the past, began to grow within her.

What started as a hobby more than 16 years ago escalated into a full-time commitment. Bear hunting is an everyday activity for Linda, taking her throughout the United States, Europe and Japan.

Her collection is dominated by the highly desirable Steiff bears of the early 1900s. Sizes of bears in Linda's collection range from a 5' tall rare Steiff bear to a tiny Schuco 2½" bear who keeps a lady's make-up compact concealed in his small body.

Her hometown of San Diego, California (and neighboring Los Angeles) benefits from her extensive travels and interests with *Linda's Teddy*

Bear, Doll & Antique Toy Festival. The popular two-day show draws over 3,000 people. It features antique and collectible Teddy Bears, Dolls and Toys by Linda and other dealers and celebrities from America and Europe.

Many organizations for children and the needy benefit from the generosity and work of numerous teddy bear clubs, groups and various organizations across the country.

Linda's shows help a local abused children's home, which has taken care of abused children since 1978. The residential treatment center sells teddy bears, donated by Linda and participating dealers and collectors at the show. Approximately $23,000 has been raised for the home since her first event.

Linda enjoys traveling and sharing her knowledge of the history of teddy bears with informative slide presentations and displays of some of the rare treasures from her collection.

Linda's most recent venture is to be a spokesperson for the teddy bear and toy company Knickerbocker Creations. She will promote and sell Knickerbocker teddy bears on national television, as well as at Disneyland® and at Walt Disney World® Teddy Bear Conventions.